THE LIFE CYCLE SERIES

Person to Person

ways of communicating

**Michael Argyle
and
Peter Trower**

D0281364

HARPER & ROW, PUBLISHERS

London   New York   Philadelphia
Hagerstown   San Francisco   Sydney

The book was devised and produced
by Multimedia Publications Inc

General Editor: *Dr. Leonard Kristal*
Prod Mgr/Art Dir/Design: *Bob Vari*
Picture Researcher: *Judy Kristal*
Illustrator: *Diana Sherman*

First published in Holland 1979 by
Multimedia Publications Inc

Published in Great Britain by
Harper & Row Ltd, 28 Tavistock Street London WC2E 7PN

British Library Cataloguing in Publication Data
Argyle, Michael
Trower, Peter
  Person to Person: ways of communicating
  References pg. 124–125
  Includes index

ISBN 00631 80979   cased
     00631 80987   paper

Colour origination: United Artists Ltd, Israel
Typeset by CCC and printed by William Clowes & Sons Limited,
Beccles and London

Contents

1 Elements of social behaviour

Human society is a network of relationships between people. If we liken the net to a fishing-net, then the knots stand for people and the string or rope for the relationships between them. But what is the rope in human affairs? Our answer is that it is communication. Mr A and Mr B can stand a few feet apart in the same room but unless they communicate there is no relationship.

Communication is what keeps people together just as surely as it is what draws them together in the first place. We believe therefore that it is one of the most important parts of human behaviour. In fact it is the part that makes all the rest of what we usually regard as human behaviour possible—because all human behaviour as we know it takes place in society.

So fundamental is communication to human living, indeed, that it goes on virtually the whole time in ways of which we are quite unconscious. If two humans come together it is virtually inevitable that they will communicate *something* to each other. So the situation which we suggested above, of two men in the same room who do not communicate, is normally impossible. The situation could not occur outside a surrealist play or painting. Even if they do not speak messages will pass between them. By their looks, expressions and body movement each will tell the other something, even if it is only, 'I don't wish to know you: keep your distance'; 'I assure you the feeling is mutual. I'll keep clear if you do.'

Rules of behaviour

How can the little signals that we send mean so much? They do so because they follow rules. Normally, to each sentence we say to somebody else there are only a few sentences that he could say in reply which would make sense. For example, if you were to say to someone, 'I think a Rolls-Royce is a classier car than a Cadillac', you would be very surprised, and not a little nonplussed, if he replied, 'My parrot can only speak Greek'. But such is the power of the rules which guide our conversations, that there is only one plausible next move for you, assuming you want to go on making sense, and that is to say something like, 'I beg your pardon', or 'What?'

Faces, arms, legs, posture—human beings communicate effectively with all of these as well as with speech.

The same rules apply to the communications that we make without words—non-verbal communication. There are many different possible expressions and movements. Some unmistakably mean one thing and one thing only. Others, however, are more subtle. To understand them we need to understand their *context*, the situation in which they are made. For instance, a quick lift of the eyebrows and brief opening of the eyes is a form of greeting that may be common to all humanity. But it can also communicate disbelief if the two people are both listening to a third, without saying anything out loud.

Person to Person is about communication: the different forms of behaviour that send messages, from the smile on your face to the clothes that you wear. Most of us learn these behaviours and use them without ever being conscious of them, just as we never stop to think how to walk. We want to let you into one of the secrets of yourself, and to show you how the net of human society is held together by the rope of social intercourse.

Many readers will find that they are as skilled at most of these behaviours as they want to be. Yet they may welcome an opportunity to brush up an isolated problem here or there, like when to look at someone in a conversation and when not to. Some will want to consider the whole message of the book in more forceful detail. They are people who lack many of the social skills that they need to take their place in society, and they are isolated, lonely and unhappy as a consequence. Some may even be labelled as mentally ill, when all that is wrong is that they have never been taught to communicate properly. In our practice as psychologists we have found that such people can be helped and their lives transformed by training in what we describe in the following pages.

Ways of communicating

Everything we do with our physical apparatus, our bodies, to communicate with other people, whether it is a wink, the wearing of a uniform or a long conversation, is social behaviour. Human bodies are very well designed for sending and receiving person-to-person messages. Two ordinary people in conversation send so many messages so rapidly that a social scientist, Ray Birdwhistell, once took 100 hours to analyse just a few seconds recorded on slow-motion film.

How do people send so many messages to each other?

By making noises

Our vocal apparatus is so sophisticated that it is capable of producing thousands of different sounds. We can make loud or soft noises by varying the force of air passing through, and vibrating, the vocal chords. We can make different tones by altering the shape of the mouth, hard and soft sounds with the use of tongue and palate, open and closed sounds by altering the aperture of the lips, high and low sounds by muscular control in the vocal chords themselves.

Putting everything into the slow dance of conversation (behind, an advertiser silently communicates his plea to buy).

Some attitudes are universal: solemn bowing means respect . . .

. . . and laughing familiarity means no respect on one side, dignity affronted on the other.

By the face

Clearly, the face is equipped with eyes for seeing, a nose for smelling and a mouth and jaw for eating—all necessary for survival. But the face has an additional and quite different function in sending social messages, and is so mobile with its complex network of muscles that it is capable of forming a large number of expressions. These expressions are made up mainly of various eyebrow positions and movements, opening and narrowing of the eyes, movement of the eyeballs and changes in the shape of the mouth.

By the body

The head, arms, and trunk. Again, people are more aware of its obvious uses, such as moving about and picking things up, than its role in communicating. This 'body talk' involves such things as positions and movements of the head and trunk, manipulation of the hands and positions of the arms and legs.

By the things we put on our bodies and by where we put them

For instance, we wear clothes to keep us warm, because unlike animals we do not have a protective covering of hair. But for the purpose of communication, we wear clothes of different colours, cut and cloth; we adorn ourselves with jewellery and other valuables, cosmetics and perfume, beards and sideburns; and we brandish pipes and walking-sticks. It matters too where we position our bodies: physically close to, or distant from, others, or in total isolation.

For efficient communication these sights and sounds have to *mean* something. In the same way that a semaphore signaller holds his flag in position and the observer reads the message, the human signaller sends specific messages to the observer. A wink may mean collusion in a secret. A raised finger may mean a rebuke. A bow means respect—unless it is done with a certain smile, in which case the opposite is meant.

Everyone sends out hundreds of these small signals in everyday conversation without being really aware of it. For instance, we may still do it when talking on the phone, even though the other person cannot see us.

It is in this way that we send out and receive a constant and complex stream of signals about what is going on inside us, our feelings, thoughts and attitudes; who we are—personality, sex, social status; and what is going on in the environment—the immediate situation, or past or future events. Few of us could begin to say what we do, and indeed if we stopped to think about it we could never do it, and yet we learn all, or nearly all of it, from birth onwards, by instruction, by observation and imitation and by being rewarded when we get it right.

After years of slow and painstaking observation of people doing various kinds of socialising and using methods such as advanced recording instruments and slow-motion film, social scientists throughout the world have identified many of the basic building blocks of human communication.

The social signals

The face
The face is the most expressive region of the body. As Gordon Allport said: 'Nature has provided it most lavishly with nerves and subtle muscles; it is unclothed and therefore the most visible region . . . it is the region where the person meets the world head-on. . . .'

'Private faces in public places . . .' registering not just private messages but the sense of group membership as well.

The fixed features of the face are the bone structure, skin, size and shape of features, and hair. Some of these we cannot do much about; others we can alter by diet, camouflage with cosmetic or tribal paint, or more radically, by cosmetic surgery. The fixed features tell us something about a person's character, race, sex, and age.

Sex

The feminine face is characterised in many people's minds with a rounded appearance such as a soft jaw-line, full 'Cupid'-shaped lips, large eyes and long lashes, and a soft and clear complexion (e.g., the 'English rose'). The masculine face has a more angular appearance such as a strong jaw-line, straight or 'boxer's nose', prominent chin and forehead, and generally rather coarser features.

Of course, not all men have classic masculine faces, nor all women feminine ones, and in real life many try to make their faces more masculine or more feminine, by make-up, hair-length, a beard and so on. Sexual stereotypes have become much more relaxed in the last few years, and the differences have become a little blurred. But the social importance of looking masculine or feminine is so great that it is doubtful whether unisex looks will ever prevail completely.

Age

In children, age is shown mainly by the changing structure of the face, and this is very rapid in the earlier years.

The later give-away signs are well known: crease-lines, especially the 'crows' feet', wrinkling of the skin, a change in complexion, loss of fatty tissue, which increases the gaunt look and sagging of the skin, and of course, balding and greying hair.

There are some things people can do to camouflage their age. Women use special skin lotions and wear cosmetics, and members of both sexes sometimes get 'face-lifts', or hair transplants, or wear wigs.

Some people look younger because of the structure of their face, such as high cheek-bones, which prevent the heavy give-away sagging under the eyes. People in hot countries age more quickly because of the effect of the sun on the skin.

Changing faces: less than 60 months separate the baby-face from the unique individual on the right below—but more than 60 years lie between Charlie (bottom left) and Sir Charles Chaplin, still recognisably the same.

Personality and personal identity

Every face is unique and the small variations in anatomical detail are greater than in any other part of the body. In addition to those features which simply identify an individual, such as bushy eyebrows or a mole on the cheek and in general the unique proportions of the face, a number of other features are generally believed to be signs of personality.

Here are some:

fat face	jolly
thin face	serious
thick lips	sexy (female)
thin lips	conscientious
high forehead	intelligent
protruding eyes	excitable
dull eyes	not alert

Research shows that there is little relationship between such detailed facial features and specific aspects of personality, although there is a very loose connection between thin, fat and muscular physiques and general personality type.

The face is capable of rapid changes in shape and colour, sometimes under our control, at other times involuntarily. The colour of a Caucasian face varies from time to time from blanched white to brightest red, changing all over or in localised areas. Although whites are generally unaware of it, blacks also vary shade similarly. The changes are due to variations in blood-flow and in the size of the blood-vessels under the skin. Because of the face's extremely complex and delicate muscles we can make several distinct brow positions, many eye and mouth shapes, and a few nose shapes. There are others. Many social signals are directly due to this facial mobility.

Feelings

We show how we feel mainly in the face, rather than in words or with any other part of the body, and if we feel an emotion strongly enough, it will automatically show itself, whether we want it to or not. In embarrassment and anger we will blush or flush, in shock or fear turn white, in extreme sadness sob, and when we are thoroughly aroused the pupils in the eye will get bigger.

Some facial expressions probably originate from our ape ancestors: for instance, opening the eyes wide in surprise in order to see better, baring the teeth in anger in order to bite. Smiling may have developed from the 'fear face' characterised by mouth corners pulled back. Ethologists believe it was used by primates as an appeasement signal. The smile has now come to mean that we have friendly intentions, though it is also used to appease.

In many cultures, people try to conceal their emotions, particularly negative ones like fear and anger, and indeed most of the time we wear the neutral interested face or the so-called social smile. Often, however, our true feelings leak out in little give-away signs, like a fleeting grimace. We also express blends of emotions, made up, for instance, of part anger and part sadness, or part happiness and part surprise.[1]

The face in conversation

A good speaker does not just say words, but is constantly moving and gesturing and above all, making rapid changes in his face. Some embellish what the speaker is saying, for example, smiling to show that it is not serious, frowning to show that it is. The good listener uses face and head signals to comment on what the speaker says: nodding, shaking, frowning, smiling or simply showing interest. These expressions are usually very rapid, often lasting only a split second. Some expressions are required by the situation: looking cheerful during greetings, solemn during church services and weddings, sorrowful at funerals. Victors in amateur sports are expected to be distinctly modest in their pleasure.

The eyes

Our eyes are probably the most intense social signallers we have. Poets have written about the bewitching speech of the eyes. One called them the windows of the soul, and we know that looks have powerful effects of extreme aggression, fear or love.

When engaged in conversation, most people look in each other's eyes for a third of the time or more, and this maintains mutual attention. When listening we watch the other person most of the time, to take in as much information as possible and because it is a basic courtesy to pay attention in this way. But when talking we do not look at the other person very much; we look at any objects relevant to the talk, or we gaze at the ceiling or floor, or out of the window. Now and then we look back to see if the other person is still listening, or dozing off, or is perhaps annoyed at what we are saying. We also use glances like passes in a sort of conversation ball game. When I have finished talking, I pass the conversation ball to you with a glance, you catch it with a mutual glance·and look away. When you pass the conversation back we do the same in reverse. It is extremely difficult to have any kind of conversation without this kind of eye-work.

Imagine someone who looks away the minute you start speaking and only looks back when you stop. Or the person who, while speaking, peers constantly and remorselessly into your eyes, or gives you shifty glances every second or so, or stares at your feet or genital area. Those who look too much cause others to feel self-conscious and uncomfortable, while people who do not look enough make others feel they are bored or disapproving. Most of us are careful about how and when we look so as not to offend others in this way.

*The eyes have it—
but can they
be read upside down?*

Friendly people look a lot more than others, and women look more than men and are, in other ways, too, rather more friendly and warm than men. Usually someone who wants to establish a closer relationship will look a lot but there is a danger that if he looks too much he will be seen as over-intimate, raising anxiety and causing the other person to withdraw. Lovers are the exception in that they gaze into each other's eyes just because they want to be intimate. Another signal of intimacy in this kind of situation is pupil dilation. Our pupils get bigger when we see someone we are fond of. Men prefer girls with larger pupils without knowing why, as experiments have shown.

There are big cultural variations in the amount of acceptable eye contact. Southern Europeans look at each other much more than Northern Europeans and Americans, and when people from these different countries meet, this often creates problems. The English think the Italians with their long looks are over-familiar, while Italians think the English cold for the reverse reason.

Dominant eyes

Increased eye contact is also a means of dominating or threatening another person. Dominant or aggressive people use a cold, hard stare to force the other person to look away. Having won this battle of the eyes, the victor may then look rather less than average at the other person. In a business hierarchy, senior people do not look at their juniors very much either. In contrast, submissive and shy people tend to avoid direct eye contact and look down a lot. Dominant male apes do very much the same things as their human counterparts, and this particular way of establishing and maintaining a peck order may have deep ancestral roots.

Does the old man want to play cat's-cradle? The child's concentrated look helps to enforce her wishes.

Eyes and personality

Your personality is also judged, rightly or wrongly, from how you use your eyes. If you are a person who makes a lot of eye contact, you are probably seen as extroverted, friendly, self-confident, natural, mature and sincere. If you avoid eye contact, you may, unfortunately, be seen less favourably—as cold, pessimistic, defensive, evasive, submissive and indifferent.[2]

Gestures

Gestures tell us much about a person; whether he is angry, anxious, lying, pleased or insecure. In doing so they may belie the spoken word or emphasise it. Some people talk with their hands, and there is a saying that Neapolitans could not speak if they were handcuffed. Deaf people and some primitive and occult communities literally talk with their hands. In conversation, we move our hands and feet to indicate to people that we are about to speak, when we start a new phrase or idea, when we fluff our words and when we want to emphasise something.

Examples:

Gesture	*Meaning*
head nod	agreement
shake fist	anger
rub palms	anticipation
clapping	approval
raise hand	attention
yawn	boredom
rub hands	cold, or delight
beckon	come
extend hand	invite to dance
point	give direction
thumb down	disapproval
fingers crossed	good luck
pat on back	encouragement, congratulations
action of shooting self	*faux pas*
outline of female body	attractive female
rub stomach	hungry
wave hand	goodbye (or a distant greeting)
shake hands	greeting

People from different countries vary greatly in the number and the types of gestures they use. Italians, especially Neapolitans, probably use the largest range, including:

palms together, hands rhythmically moved up and down	begging
striking the forehead	disappointment
pressing the region of the heart	sincerity
tapping nose	suspicion
thumbs against temples, hands open	taunting
flicking the chin	bribery

Another group which uses many gestures are the Arabs. They use:

backward jerk of head, clicking noise with tongue	'no'
striking thighs and rocking while seated	distress
fingers poised, pointing up, hand moving up and down	go slowly

Posture

The great American psychologist William James was the first to discover nearly fifty years ago the importance of posture in communicating attitudes. He took thirty photographs of people in which the head, trunk, feet, knees and arms were systematically varied, and he asked volunteers to say what attitudes were being expressed. Four main postures emerged:

(a) approach—an attentive posture communicated by a forward lean of the body;

(b) withdrawal—a negative posture communicated by drawing back or turning away;

(c) expansion—a proud, conceited, arrogant or disdainful posture communicated by an expanded chest, erect or backward-leaning trunk, erect head and raised shoulders;

(d) contraction—a depressed, downcast, or dejected posture communicated by a forward-leaning trunk, a bowed head, drooping shoulders and a sunken chest.

Today we describe these attitudes as warm, cold, dominant, and submissive. More realistic and sophisticated research in recent years has gone quite a long way towards substantiating James's findings. Albert Mehrabian, working in California, has found another way of expressing dominance: a relaxed, seated posture, leaning backward or sideways with sprawled and relaxed limbs. He also found that a more tidy posture, with feet, knees and hands together added to a timid impression.[3]

Posture giveaways: the relaxed group confidence of the men challenges the passing girl— who dissociates herself from it.

Simple greeting or status demonstration?

Psychoanalysts have made quite different interpretations of posture, seeing them as more related to inner conflicts, especially to do with sex. The following examples are not based on research findings!

no movement in pelvis	sexual inhibition
stiff military bearing (males)	imprisoned
prim and upright (females)	anxiety
affected bearing	conflict between flirtation and shyness
shoulders forward, chest deflated (girl)	ashamed of breast development
nestling into chair, languid, erotic manner	expresses sexual impulses

Some societies have more extravagant ways of expressing various attitudes. For instance, the Batoka express humility by throwing themselves on their backs, rolling from side to side, slapping the outsides of their thighs. This means, 'You need not subdue me, I am subdued already'. The ancient Peruvians did it by walking about with hands bound and a rope around their necks. The Fundah and Tonga allow someone to place a foot on their heads, while Europeans drop their arms and sigh.

Use of space

There is a limit to how far two people can be apart and yet hear and see each other. Within that limit, their distance from each other depends on the way they feel and their relative status. A

Westerners would not feel comfortable as close to one another as these Arabs: personal territorial demands are larger here.

16

great deal of early research on the use of space was carried out by Edward T. Hall.[4]

We each have a kind of personal space around us into which only certain people are allowed. Only our spouses, lovers, young children and close family are permitted within eighteen inches—the intimate space. At this distance we can touch each other nearly all over, smell and feel each other's body odours, heat and breath, and see the smallest pores and blemishes in each other's skin.

We allow friends within between eighteen inches and four feet—the personal space. From four to nine feet—the social space—we conduct most of our social relationships. At this distance we cannot touch or smell each other and cannot see the give-away details of appearance.

Distances greater than this are regarded as public and completely impersonal. There are situations where this system is abandoned; for example, in crowded places like trains where people studiously avoid any exchange of social signals.

Another way we use space is by turning our bodies towards or away from each other. Face-to-face orientation together with physical closeness makes for extreme intimacy, and most of us avoid it by, for instance, looking away if a person comes too close on a crowded train. While friends generally like to sit close and at right angles or side-by-side for conversation, competitors prefer to sit opposite and further away.

People use the space around them as their private territory, much as animals do. While animals leave markings, droppings or urine, as a territorial warning to predators, humans use clothes, furniture, names on doors and other belongings. A high-status businessman may use a large table and chair for himself and small chairs for his visitors as a way of using space—distance and height—to dominate. A judge sits on his bench and a priest stands in his pulpit. A low-status person shows deference by keeping at a respectful distance, entering the territory of a higher-status person with trepidation—a soft knock on the door, a pause inside the door, then a pause while waiting to be told whether to stand or sit. The high-status person may walk straight in, *behind* the other's desk and stand over him, in order to emphasise his dominance.

People form themselves into social groups, at parties for instance, by using these distance and orientation cues. They form a circle or semi-circle, stand or sit close and orient themselves towards each other. They may jut out elbows, shoulders, legs and feet, so that most people will walk round the group as if there is some magic barrier surrounding its members.

The use of space varies according to different cultures. Arabs and Latin Americans like to stand directly facing each other and closer than North Americans or Europeans. Black Americans prefer even more space between them. In parts of India, different castes traditionally had to keep the following distances from each other:

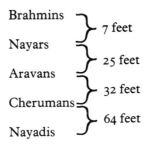

Brahmins	
	7 feet
Nayars	
	25 feet
Aravans	
	32 feet
Cherumans	
	64 feet
Nayadis	

Touching

Touching is probably the most primitive and intimate form of personal involvement possible, often of a sexual kind. In some Western cultures touching is so taboo that personal space is seldom invaded. One scientist carried out a survey of the rate of touching as it varies from country to country. In several countries he sat down in cafés and recorded how often people touched each other in one hour. He found the following:

San Juan (Puerto Rico)	180
Paris	110
Gainesville (Florida)	2
London	0

There are forms of touching which do not signal intimacy, and these are commonly allowed between strangers. Professionals such as doctors, nurses, tailors, dentists, masseurs, gymnasts, instructors, barbers, beauticians and shoe salesmen may touch. It is allowed in some games, as in rugby and wrestling. It is allowed in some ceremonies, such as graduation, wedding and healing ceremonies, in greetings. On crowded underground trains and other public places it is ignored rather than allowed.

Many people in Europe and America have come to feel so deprived of the intimacy of touching that they form special groups to explore and encourage close, if temporary, relationships through touch and other means.

Physical appearance

Clothes, decorations, physique, hair and facial features convey much information about us. Strict rules govern the clothes we wear. We do not, for instance, wear football boots with a dinner-jacket, or a boiler suit to work in an insurance office. A worker in an office in the City of London or on Wall Street will wear more formal dress than someone in a similar job in a country town.

Young people often feel the need to identify with a peer group and in the last two decades in Britain there have been a number of youth movements with distinct uniforms—teddy boys, mods, rockers, skinheads, hippies and punks.

People also choose particular clothes to project their personalities. Sociable and extroverted types wear brighter and more saturated colours than more introverted and reserved people. Some people wear odd combinations of clothes to express their individuality. For instance, someone might convey an impression

'Clothes oft proclaim . . .'
that this man wishes to
show he is a rule-breaker.

18

A 'uniform' proclaims membership of a group or class—and need not necessarily mean clothes!

of high social status, eccentricity, Scottish origin and bad temper, by an expensive suit with gold cufflinks, luminous green socks, a beret, tartan tie and bushy red beard.

The voice

Apart from the *visual* elements of behaviour and appearance, there is the *auditory* one, comprising particularly the use of the voice. For intelligible speech, our voice must be loud enough for the other to hear, clear enough for him to distinguish the words, and at a reasonable speed so that he can follow what we are saying. Beyond that, we vary the sounds to express feelings and attitudes and use sounds as an auditory version of punctuation.

Volume

Most research has shown that a louder voice is used by more assertive people and expresses certain strong feelings like anger, surprise and fear. Conversely, soft volume is adopted both by shy and by warm people, who differ from each other in tone and pitch. We also use volume to emphasise what we are saying.

Tone

Tone or voice quality depends on the way the sound produced in the vocal chords echoes in the hollows of the mouth and nose. Resonant sounds are the most attractive to listen to, and combine with a loud voice to produce a dominant impression, and with a soft volume to give an impression of sadness or affection. A throaty voice sounds mature and sophisticated, a flat voice sounds depressed and flabby, a hollow voice weak, and a breathy voice anxious.

Pitch

As you might expect, low-pitched voices sound masculine, high ones feminine, but related to this—and with apologies to feminists and men with high-pitched voices—low ones are thought to sound more dominant, high ones more submissive. A pitch that varies a lot sounds feminine too, but findings on what else it shows are contradictory. Some research shows that a varied pitch suggests a dynamic, pleasant and happy person, but another recent study found that varied pitch gave an impression of a cruel, serious and unemotional creature. Whatever it means in or to different people, pitch variation is important in giving meaning, colour and emphasis to speech. A lack of variation is characteristic of depression. When people speak both fast and loudly, we may think they are persuasive and impressive.

On the other hand Charles Aronovitch found that most people think a booming voice and rapid rate of speech in fact conceal the cautious introvert, full of self-doubts and probably immature. Observers presumably think that the loud, rapid talker is trying to cover up these weaknesses. Many other feelings and attitudes can be detected by the sound of the voice. For instance, anxious people may speak very fast with a lot of speech errors such as stuttering. A person also reveals his social class in speech—and not only by his accent. Middle-class accents are supposed not only to be the best but to have more clarity with less variation and stumbling over words.

Speech

Ideally, two people in conversation each talk about 50 per cent of the time. In practice, however, this varies from about 70 to 30 per cent for each partner, with notable exceptions, like interviewing. Really boring people or those who are very withdrawn or depressed go outside those ranges—about 90 per cent and 10 per cent respectively. A lot of speech is designed just to give factual information, but it is also used to do a lot of other things, which recent research has helped us to understand better.

One kind of speech is designed not for exchanging information but for getting people to do things. Army officers do not gossip with their men but give commands, orders and instructions. This special use of language is probably also one of the earliest that children learn in order to get food and toys. It is much used by dominant people. A related kind of speech is questioning. This common verbal technique is more useful and versatile than many may realise. It is practically guaranteed to get the other person to say something and is most effective at getting conversations going and showing interest.

Do as you're told!
Volume means
command.

Chat or gossip is a very inefficient form of speech to use for exchanging information or getting people to do things. It has only recently been fully realised, however, that this is not what chat is for. Its main use is simply a means of enjoying a relationship. It probably replaces grooming in primates, so that while monkeys touch each other, pick fleas and grunt, humans mostly chat.

Often repeated phrases in everyday speech do not really mean anything in themselves but rather *do* something—that is, they bring about some change in the immediate situation. Take greetings: these highly ritualised forms of words do not tell you anything, but they are another sort of verbal grooming. Farewells and giving thanks are two other examples which serve a similar purpose.

2 The two languages of humans

Humans use two quite separate languages, each with its own function. We are all familiar with verbal or spoken language, be it Hindi or English, or any other used to exchange information about the world. This is the language of facts and things, the spoken language of logic and problem-solving, the language that can be written down. There is another more mysterious language called body *language, which is often used quite unconsciously to express the truly human bits of ourselves—feelings, attitudes and personality. Computers do sums and write a kind of English, but this other language is beyond machines. Man needs both languages to express the two sides to his being: his human side involving relationships with other people, and his practical, businesslike side of getting things done.*

Human relationships are established, developed and maintained mainly by non-verbal signals, although of course words are also used. A number of experiments have shown that if an unfriendly message is delivered in a friendly tone of voice and with a smiling face, the contents of the message are largely discounted by adults, and the message is thought to be friendly.[1] This works rather differently for children, who are sensitive to negative verbal messages, such as, 'I'm afraid you've been very naughty', even if said in a pleasant tone of voice and with a smile.

We are only partly aware of non-verbal signals from others; we are quite unaware of their pupils expanding when attracted to us and do not usually notice their posture. In addition, we are hardly ever aware of the signals we are sending ourselves. These non-verbal signals constitute a 'silent language', which although they may be the more important aspect of an encounter, operate largely outside the focus of conscious attention. Two young people in love may talk about mathematics, or religion. This is obviously not their main concern but they have to talk about *something*.

When two people are carrying out a joint manual task, like cutting down a tree, or when one supervises another, words are more useful for sending detailed information, solving problems and arriving at decisions. It is generally assumed that language evolved because it gave an evolutionary advantage in such

*He doesn't need
to shout 'I've won!'—
his body tells us
he's exultant.*

practical situations. Non-verbal signals are also used: for example, pointing and other gestures, helping, guiding, facial comments. In noisy factories and in broadcasting studios where speech is impossible, these partly take the place of speech. Signals of this kind are not the same as body language.

Signs and signals, not body language. However she's dressed, that thumb means 'I want a lift'.

Social skills

Social behaviour is like driving a car. The analogy may strike you as odd, but it is true in two important ways. Both have goals: a car driver sets out to go somewhere, and so, in effect, does someone in a social interaction. Both are skilled performances, at which some people are better than others.

The goal of a car journey is usually very definite, like, say going from London to Plymouth. Even when the target is as clear as this, people vary in how methodical they are about getting there. Some drivers will sit down beforehand with a map and work out every stage of the route in detail, where to turn right and where left, where there may be traffic jams to avoid, the number of an exit from the motorway and so on. Others will work out only the first few miles and make up a route as they go along.

Many car trips have a less specific goal—to find a pub or a beach that one has not tried before. Here again it is possible to work out a complete route in advance. But that takes away half the pleasure, that of exploring the unknown. The goal is a double one; to go where one has not been before and to select from among the unfamiliar pubs the one that looks most congenial. Finally, there is the Sunday afternoon driver, who is not going anywhere but just passing time in pleasant scenery.

Conversations rarely have quite such neat goals. Even if you set out to agree with your wife a menu for a party, or to negotiate a manning agreement in a factory, the goal moves as you get close to it. Nonetheless, you know the general direction, and you will recognise your goal, whether it is Plymouth, a menu or an acceptable agreement.

Many conversations are more like the search for the unknown pub. Interviews to select a new assistant manager, the early stages of courtship, or 'chatting up', fit this model, and so do the periods of small talk that really conceal an attempt to find out something like whether your neighbour's jam is better, or children's bicycles more expensive, than yours, or whether your salesman friend who works for a rival company has sold more than you in the past month.

Real small talk is like the Sunday scenic ride, goalless and undertaken for its own sake. Like the unplanned car trip it can provide moments of great surprise and pleasure, but often ends up fruitless and boring.

Among the different types of conversational 'journey', each with its own goal, are the following. One type is simply used to convey information, such as teaching or training someone.

The pupil's limbs become 'servo-mechanisms' controlled by the movements of the instructor: direct communication.

Another type is designed for solving problems and taking decisions, as in committee meetings. Another aims to get to know someone and to enjoy a relationship, as in chat and gossip.

Steering a conversation successfully is like navigating a car, reading the signs from the road and countryside and comparing them with your map. If you do not know your right from your left, north from south, or the difference between a first-class and a second-class road, you will be in trouble. Similarly, if you cannot recognise the signs and signals that the other person or people in your conversations send out, you will have difficulty in reaching your goal.[2]

Conversation as skill

When you first sit behind the steering-wheel of a car there seems to be the most enormous amount to do. Just to keep the car going in a straight line takes a concentrated effort, without worrying about speed, changing gear, turning corners or signalling. All the separate operations that make up driving a car have to be learned separately and put together. Later you can brake and change gear without thinking as you read the road sign at an unfamiliar junction (as long as the situation is not too complicated). A very experienced driver can negotiate a familiar route without consciously thinking what he is doing.

It is longer sequences of behaviour that are affected by a person's private way of thinking about things. A school-teacher's behaviour is affected by her training: she has a plan for the lesson, she may be trying to ask 'higher-order questions' by raising more general or fundamental issues, and she has ideas about what behaviour by pupils is acceptable. The pupils have a different view of the classroom: if the teacher breaks *their* rules she has to be punished, e.g., if she sets too much homework or is unfair the class creates more noise and disorder.[3]

Highly developed skills tend to impose a standard repertoire of behaviour on their practitioners.

Feedback

A motorist has to watch the road continually, so that he can make rapid corrective action with the steering-wheel, the brakes and gears, etc. This continuous adjustment in response to feedback is an essential part of skilled behaviour. Social performance also depends on feedback. If we see that another person hasn't understood, we explain the point more clearly; if we see someone getting bored or hostile, we try to do something about it. An inexperienced driver often makes his corrections too late, he sees the car is about to hit something so he swings the wheel round. The skilled motorist acts sooner, his adjustments will be more accurate—and he makes them without thinking. Similarly, the trainee interviewer might discover after several minutes that the candidate is saying very little; so he will take corrective action, which might consist of asking open-ended questions like 'what sort of work did you do in your last job?' which opens the way to a long answer. Or he may give encouragement when the other does speak; he smiles, nods, looks and makes approving noises. This may lead to the candidate talking all the time, so that further corrective action is needed. The skilled interviewer, on the other hand, can get a candidate talking the right amount within the first few seconds of the interview.

Feedback in a conversation comes from looking at the other's facial expression, and also from what the other person says and the way that he says it. His non-verbal sounds, 'uh-huh', and meaningless phrases like 'really?' and 'I see' are more important for feedback than words.

By laughing, the teacher gives the children an appropriate response to mimic—and because laughter means approval, reinforces the lesson.

When dealing with a car we don't have to think about the car's feelings or wonder if the car approves of us. When dealing with people, however, we *are* concerned with their reactions and how we imagine they see us. This happens particularly when a person is being interviewed, appearing in public, or in front of a TV camera. People who are good at judging how others are reacting are more effective at social behaviour. Mental patients are so absorbed in themselves and their problems that they do not bother about what others are thinking.

Sequences of social behaviour

When we perform a simple physical skill we must know what to do to produce the effect we desire—which oar to use to make a rowing-boat turn left, or how to make the car go faster and slower. There are a number of these cause-and-effect sequences in social behaviour and these are implicitly known and used by all but the socially inadequate.

Reinforcement

Response matching between two cronies greeting each other.

Suppose Joan wants George to take more interest in the children. If Joan rewards any kind of behaviour of George by smiles, head-nods, looking, touching or approving noises, George will rapidly increase his production of that behaviour. If Joan frowns, looks

Same signal—but one patronises as well as encourages, the other says a weary 'Thanks'.

away, or makes disapproving noises, George stops whatever he was doing. Joan can choose whether to reward George more for one kind of behaviour than another. By such methods she may be able to increase the amount George talks about the children, and reduce the amount he talks about his work, or golf. The effect is quite rapid. It often takes less than a minute and it can occur without George being aware of it. Joan may not be aware of it either, but expresses her spontaneous approval or disapproval of George's behaviour. The effect works in both directions, for when Joan does what George wants, he rewards her for rewarding him, so he will be modifying Joan's behaviour too. This is one of the main ways in which people accommodate to one another—by modifying each other's behaviour in the direction of what is wanted. A person will have a greater influence of this kind if he emits strong signals of approval and disapproval, as opposed to producing neither, or approving of everything, for example.

It has been found that popular people are very rewarding, while unpopular people and most mental patients are very unrewarding, because they are more concerned with trying to obtain rewards for themselves. In order to be liked, indeed, to maintain relationships at all, we must give more rewards than punishments.

Response-matching

Very often in a social situation one person produces very similar behaviour to another's. He may adopt a similar posture, follow the other's smiles and head-nods, or non-verbal signals. He may even use similar styles of speech—loudness, accent, length of remark, or tendency to interrupt—and may use similar words. This process is usually unconscious. Indeed when we become aware that it is happening we may feel self-conscious and false to our true selves, and we may try to stop it. Deliberate response-matching can sometimes be used deliberately. It can help, for example, to calm a person who is very nervous by acting very calmly. If you try this you must be in firm control of yourself, for there is a danger of catching his anxiety. A person who is aware of these processes, however, will be able to impose his mood on the other.

Listeners can flatter a speaker—and keep him speaking—by adopting his gestures.

Accommodation

When two or more people engage in social behaviour they adapt their own personal styles to fit in with each other. They have to agree on an activity or topic of conversation. They must work out how much of the time each person speaks. This negotiation is done by means of interruptions and non-verbal signals like head-nods. They also have to agree on a level of intimacy and who is to be dominant, which are also negotiated by non-verbal signals. All these relations may change during the course of the encounter, or a series of encounters, as the relationship develops.

Rules

It would be impossible to play a game if one person thought he was playing bridge while another believed he was playing whist. Similarly, a social encounter would be awkward if some people thought they were at a party, while others thought it was a committee meeting. For social behaviour to proceed, everyone must agree on the nature of the situation, and keep to the same rules. If a person wants to learn to play tennis he must learn both the particular skills needed and the rules of the game. Human society develops rules which people are expected to keep. We follow many rules without being aware of what the rules are. We speak without really thinking about the rules of grammar.

Many of the rules of behaviour do vary between situations— for example, the rules of behaviour at dinner-parties as opposed to pubs or concerts. Rules for a particular situation often vary between cultures: for example, the rules governing buying and selling, and behaviour at meals. Some rules, however, appear to be universal to most situations and cultures. For example, questions should lead to answers, and people should take turns to speak.

No rules, no game!

3 Judging other people-believing is seeing

John is introduced to a stranger at a party. He notices that the man wears spectacles and has a high forehead and smiles, and from this he assumes the man is intelligent and well-adjusted. He also notices he is well-built, and this suggests to him that he is adventurous and self-reliant. The stranger's tallness suggests leadership and ability to get on. When the man speaks, John notices his 'refined' accent and assumes he is upper-class and has a high-status job.

John is not alone in making such glib and often false assumptions. In new situations, where we have little information, we all tend to notice very obvious things about strangers. From physical appearance and other superficial clues we make inferences that are often unjustified.[1]

Research has shown that we see a physically attractive stranger as possessing all sorts of favourable qualities, such as being sexually warmer and more responsive, sensitive, kind, interesting, strong, sociable and so on.

This means that attractive-looking people get favours and privileges that are denied to the less attractive. This has some disturbing implications. One American psychologist, David Landy, set up a make-believe courtroom with simulated judges and defendants whose guilt was not in doubt. He found that an unattractive defendant was sentenced to over nine years compared with an attractive one who received only six and a half years. Others carried out similar experiments with similar results. While this does not mean that this happens in real courts, it makes us aware of the possibilities.

The physical clues that affect judgements of others in this way include body-build and height, clothes, skin colour and structural features of the face. How is it that people leap to such conclusions without better evidence? It is partly because we carry around in our heads certain stereotypes that are popular in the culture. Even if we do not believe it rationally, we may be influenced by the idea that all blondes are dumb, 'dizzy', innocent and so on, and when we see a blonde we may attribute to her all these characteristics—and behave towards her accordingly. A stereotype, then, is a simplified belief about a particular group of people, a belief that everyone in that group is roughly the same.

Stripped of their identifying uniforms, what judgements can we make about people like this? Tramps or bankers? Fun or misery? Rebels or conformists?

Stereotypes are a major source of prejudice, and they operate most strongly when ignorance is greatest. For instance, if you are not acquainted with a West Indian or a Jew, you are more likely to think in stereotypes than if you know one of them well.

Some stereotypes are shared by a whole community, but some are unique to one individual. Someone may have a paranoid belief that particular groups are against him. Some anxious people see all strangers as threatening. These stereotypes are often the result of experiences with a few people. For example, a girl who receives sexual advances from the first two or three men she goes out with may fall in quickly with the belief that 'men are only interested in sex'.

A second type of inference does not use stereotypes, but our own private personality theories. These often bear little relation to reality and can mislead us as much as stereotypes. For instance, psychologist L. Chelsea asked one group of girls to judge another group on a number of personality traits. All the girl judges thought that boldness and extroversion were strongly related. If they rated a girl as very extroverted, they also rated her as very bold. It was found, however, that there was no relationship between these two traits at all. The girl judges were distorting reality to fit in with their own beliefs.

Few of the personality traits that we assume to be related are actually linked. Many psychologists nowadays believe that personality traits, where they exist at all, operate in a complex way, in combination with the demands of situations. They are largely convenient myths which help us to think simply, but not reliably, about other people. Many studies have shown that people are not as consistent in their behaviour as a personality theory would have us believe, but we go on believing in personality because it makes the world a more secure and predictable place.

If stereotypes and personality judgements are unreliable, surely we are on safer ground with judgements of abilities, such as intelligence? Not always, it appears. Jerry Wiggins gave people brief case histories of college students and asked them to estimate the students' intelligence. Two-thirds of the judges used vocabulary and social achievement as the basis for their estimates, which were in fact the best indicators. But others used social status and industriousness in making their judgements; while a few used very odd criteria, such as emotional instability, as the sole indicator of high intelligence.

There is a common and often false belief that first impressions about a person are the right ones and should be trusted. 'I knew he was a shady character from the first time I met him,' people say. Some first impressions do tend to stick. In one experiment by Edward Jones, people watched a stranger solve some problems, though he got some of the later ones wrong. They also watched another man get problems wrong to start with, but then get the rest right. Which was seen as the most intelligent? Most people thought the first man, even though both men got the same proportion of problems right in the end.

But first impressions are not always the same as the last ones. People who wear glasses are seen as more intelligent if they are seen briefly, doing nothing in particular. But if we have a chance to listen to them talk, even for five minutes, the wearing of spectacles has no effect at all on our judgement.

When dealing with strangers and people we do not know well, we supply information from our own beliefs, even though they are often unreliable, to make up for gaps in our knowledge. However, as we get to know people better, we gather more information about them and are able to make judgements rather than guesses about them. As we build up a picture from the stable background characteristics, we begin to see more clearly the changes in mood, emotion and motive, and these become the features that interest us day to day.

For him it was lust at first sight, for her he was worth a second glance. But will either really be what they think they see in each other?

Impressions and judgements

Let is now consider some of the judgements we make about each other,[2] and the sort of information we draw upon to make them. One group of judgements is about *stable* attributes—personality, abilities, beliefs, attitudes, and habits.

We call these attributes stable because we assume they are continuous properties of the person, though they may not always be openly manifest. We come to believe in stable attributes only after seeing a person on a number of different occasions, or getting reliable information from other observers.

Interpersonal attitudes

There is a difference between our attitudes to people present in an immediate situation, and our attitudes in general to, say, politicians or Roman Catholics. We express or reveal our interpersonal attitudes towards another when (a) we adopt the appropriate non-verbal behaviour of, say, friendliness or dominance; and (b) if we behave that way consistently in the presence of the other; but only (c) if our behaviour is not attributable to another cause, such as our personality or an ulterior motive. For instance, if someone smiles at you and leans forward and makes positive comments about you in the office and the pub, but does not also do this with everyone else, you have good reason to think, 'He likes me!'—but not if you have just won a fortune.

Friendly within groupings, these groups do not mingle or signal to one another although all are doing the same thing.

*It is easier to relate
to a stranger who wears
at least one badge—
here it is colour—of
the group you belong to.*

Cultural groups and social roles

This information comes from facts we glean about the other person either in conversation with him from other people who know him, or by means of direct observation.

Emotion and mood

There are two main sources of information for these non-stable attributes. We draw conclusions from verbal and non-verbal signals, particularly from the face (especially the brows, eyes and mouth), voice inflections, volume and pitch, and bodily movements (particularly of the hands), and, of course, people sometimes say what they feel. Secondly, we try to discover a reason for the feeling. If someone has just won the pools or a beauty contest we will believe he is happy or pleased even if he or she does not show it.

Moods are rather different, in that the cause may not be obvious nor related to the conversation. Moods are detected mainly from behaviour.

*Behaviour tells us what
the mood is: nobody
here is going
to burst into tears.*

Motives

We may attribute behaviour to a motive as soon as we believe that the motive has become obvious. Sometimes we attribute an ulterior motive to someone because we know him and know that he often has hidden reasons. At other times we may need clues from several different areas of behaviour to lead us to believe a person has a particular motive.

Mistaken beliefs about causes of behaviour

Making an incorrect guess about the cause of another's behaviour can be the cause of faulty judgement. For instance, John is upset because Steve has been rather short with him in the tea-room. John thinks he was the cause of Steve's bad temper—but he has overlooked other possible causes: that it was Steve's personality (he is always bad tempered); he was in a bad mood (has a hangover); was angry (told off by the boss) and so on.

Mistaking rules and roles

When a person overlooks the rules of a situation and the roles of the participants, behaviour can be misinterpreted. For instance, officials such as policemen, doctors, bank managers, receptionists, are expected to behave in a businesslike way—but this does not mean they are being unfriendly. And a friendly stranger arouses suspicion.

Too impulsive or forceful a display of affection from a stranger causes suspicion.

Deception and camouflage

Even the most honest of us at times actively try to deceive each other. In Western society it is socially unacceptable to show negative emotions and attitudes in public. People therefore wear socially-sanctioned expressions almost like masks, and it takes the perceptive observer to see through them. How does the good observer see through these masks?

He watches those parts of the face and body people *don't* control very well. For instance, Paul Ekman and Wallace Friesen have shown that people control their mouths easily, but not the region of the eyes and forehead. We often give away our true feelings in a fleeting expression like a grimace, before controlling it. A false smile is detectable when it is switched on and off too quickly, or it appears around the mouth, but not the eyes, which may be narrowed as in anger.

'Leakage' of feeling also occurs in the voice. Fear is accompanied by variable volume and pitch and an upward inflection at the end of sentences. The hands also give powerful cues; gripping the hands together, touching and hiding the face indicate anxiety.

Absent or conflicting information and cues

Lack of information about someone can be a source of mistaken judgements, as we have seen. Experiments show that we judge emotion much more accurately if we know the cause and situation. But what happens if the non-verbal expression and situation are apparently contradictory? When a person smiles while watching a hanging, does it mean that he is happy? Most people try to explain the smile away, reasoning that he was probably smiling because the hanged man was an enemy, or he was covering up his true feelings. We may send ambiguous or double messages, such as 'Of course I love you, dear', said in a hostile manner. One rule is that the non-verbal signals communicate the true feeling, but this is more likely to be true when they are negative, since we often pretend to be happy or friendly.

Leaking information: the girl is amused— but by something she feels is really no laughing matter.

The importance of good observation

Studies have shown that people who are sensitive and accurate observers of others are popular and can become leaders. Women are generally better than men at understanding what other people feel—partly because they look more and seem to be more interested in human relations. It has also been found that people make better judgements of those who are similar to themselves in age, sex, social class and cultural background. This is probably because they have more experience with people like themselves, are sensitive to the relevant cues and interpret them correctly. This is akin to the ability to take the role of the other: to metaphorically step into his shoes. If John can take the role of Steve, he will be better able to predict what Steve will do and act accordingly. Exercises like role-reversal, where we act out each other's roles, are often used to help improve this skill.

Incorrect judgements about people can lead to misunderstanding and breakdowns of relationships at all levels—budding friendships, marriages and families, business and professional relationships, and on a wider scale, between whole communities of people. How do these judgements come about?

Stereotypes and private beliefs

We have already seen that stereotypes and our own 'personality theories' are often false. Some of the errors of judgement associated with them can have very serious, even tragic consequences—from the Nazis' ideas about Jews to the suicide who believes that nobody wants her.

Classic victims of 'stereotyping': Nazis said Jews were 'all the same'. Such tendencies can begin very early (below): blacks and whites already prefer to play with reflections of their own stereotypes.

Failures in detection and identification of cues

If we fail to observe subtle non-verbal cues other people give about their emotional states and attitudes, we make incorrect judgements about them. For instance, politeness or friendliness can be mistaken for sexual interest and sadness for hostility.

Distortions in interpreting the actions of others[3]

Our moods, attitudes and goals can have a strong effect on the way we identify the actions of others. S. Feshbach and R. D. Singer found that subjects who had been put in a state of fear by electric shock judged photographs of faces as more fearsome and aggressive. We tend to see our environment through the spectacles of our moods. If we are anxious, we interpret things as threatening; if angry, as insulting or persecuting; if depressed, we may see people's actions as due to our deficiencies while, if we are elated and confident, we tend to interpret events as due to our qualities.

Our attitudes also colour our interpretations. If we like someone, we tend to see them as possessing all sorts of favourable qualities, and interpret what they do in that light. Conversely, if we dislike someone, nothing they do is seen as favourable.

Finally, our interpretations may be influenced by our goals, our motivations. For example, if we do badly in an examination, we may attribute this to bad teaching, or to an unfairly set paper, rather than to our own laziness or lack of ability. By attributing the cause of failures to others we can avoid the loss of self-esteem, the sense of failure that doing badly in an exam would entail. Similarly, if a person we are talking to in a social situation looks ill at ease, we can avoid feeling socially incompetent by attributing it to another cause, such as his shyness. On the other hand, if an attractive stranger smiles at us, we are also more likely to interpret that smile as due to their liking us than to other causes, because this is rewarding to us.

Mime succeeds because of careful exaggeration of the non-verbal cues which identify what we do and feel.

4 Analysing conversation

At school we are taught vocabulary, grammar and other aspects of written language. The art of conversation we pick up at home, in the playground, in the street and in our day-to-day encounters with others. We gradually learn how to string words together, and how to use gestures, movement, facial expressions and vocalisations to punctuate, emphasise, clarify and colour the things we say. We become familiar with literally hundreds of different kinds of conversations suitable for various situations—at home, with friends, at work, in shops, at parties and dances and so on. In a small town in Kansas one study found that, overall, the people knew how to conduct themselves appropriately in no less than 800 different situations, each of which demanded its own type of conversation, designed for a special task or purpose.

The rules of conversation

Suppose that John is telling Jill about his day at the office. His talk consists of a number of remarks or utterances. By an utterance we mean any string of spoken words, before and after which the speaker is silent. If the utterance is long, John may say more than one kind of thing : he may answer a question and then ask another one back, involving two pieces of behaviour. He may say several things in this way, building up quite a complex utterance. At the same time John will also send many non-verbal signals. His tone of voice, facial expressions and gestures elaborate the meaning of the utterance and indicate when it is about to end. Many utterances are ambiguous or meaningless without these further signals.

Since it takes two to make conversation, each partner must 'mesh' smoothly with the other so that they are not both talking or silent at the same time. This is a basic rule. John's and Jill's utterances should follow one another without much pause or overlap. If there are long delays interspersed with interruptions there will probably be embarrassment or conflict between them.

A range of pauses up to a second or two is normal. Short interruptions are also normal, as when someone is eager to speak. A listener may help a speaker to finish a sentence or make a comment, like 'that's interesting', which is not intended to stop the other person speaking. Some people like long leisurely silences and hate interruptions, which jar their nerves. Others like

*Very different people
can conduct satisfactory
conversations, provided
they stick to the rules.*

conversations to be more high-powered, quick-fire affairs and don't mind the interruptions. People with different temperaments who normally speak at different paces must make quite large efforts to compromise and mesh or they will feel that they are just not suited to each other.

The turn-taking is not done verbally ('I've finished—your turn'), but by a system of mainly non-verbal cues.

When a speaker is coming to the end of his sentence he starts a long look at the other person, stops gesturing, returns his hands to rest, and lowers the pitch of his voice on the last word or two. If someone wants to speak he makes rapid head-nods and shows other signs of impatience. If he wants to keep the floor he avoids looking up at the ends of sentences and keeps a hand in mid-gesture.[1]

There is often competition for the floor. For instance, if John interrupts, Paul may counter by increasing the volume of his voice; John may do the same, and Paul may try to speak louder still. The pair eventually settle down to a rhythm, each speaking a certain proportion of the time, depending on the outcome of some of these early struggles for the floor. Once this rhythm between two people has developed and stabilised, it will endure for a long time, perhaps months or years.

People adapt to each other in conversation in many other ways. For instance, a listener reacts to the content of what the speaker says, looking sympathetic at the sad parts, smiling in the funny parts, and so on. They also engage in what has been called a 'gestural dance', swaying backwards and forwards in synchrony and mirroring each other's gestures.

Conversation imposes mutual adaptation on its participants.

What we say in conversations

When people converse, they do not make statements at random, but follow certain rules which work rather like the rules of grammar in formal language.

The rules of conversation are taken very much for granted. We are only aware of them if they are broken. Take the following as examples:

Jill: Did you have a good day at the office dear?
John: How's your mother?
Jill: Yes.

or

Jill: Morning John—How are you?
John: No, they're in the kitchen.

There is obviously something strange here. We can try to explain it by looking for something wrong in their relationship, or think they must be playing a strange game, or that one or both of them must be mad. But it is clear that since certain rules are being broken therefore they must exist. Some rules come immediately to mind. Questions are nearly always followed by answers. But there are different kinds of question and different kinds of answer. When we ask for advice we expect to receive advice. When we make a request for action, we expect compliance or refusal. Robert Bales studied groups of people talking and found a considerable degree of regularity in their responses to each other. For example, if one person in the group asked for information or guidance, someone would nearly always give it. If someone joked and laughed, another would reciprocate.

JILL: *Did you have a good day?*
JOHN: *How's your mother?*
Break the rules and you lose the sense.

The more we find out about these predictable patterns or rules of talk, the more help we can give to people who feel hopeless at making conversation. This is why social scientists are aiming for a more thorough understanding. Some scientists have managed to program computers to talk to each other, or to a real person. One such program, called ELIZA, was developed about ten years ago at the Massachusetts Institute of Technology in America. The following is the transcript between a human and ELIZA, who 'talks' in capitals.[2]

Men are all alike.
IN WHAT WAY?
They're always bugging us about something or other.
CAN YOU THINK OF A SPECIFIC EXAMPLE?
Well, my boyfriend made me come here.
YOUR BOYFRIEND MADE YOU COME HERE?
He says I'm depressed much of the time.
I AM SORRY TO HEAR YOU ARE DEPRESSED.
It's true. I am unhappy.
DO YOU THINK COMING HERE WILL HELP YOU NOT TO BE UNHAPPY?
I need some help, that much seems certain.
WHAT WOULD IT MEAN TO YOU IF YOU GOT SOME HELP?
Perhaps I could learn to get along with my mother.
TELL ME MORE ABOUT YOUR FAMILY.
My mother takes care of me.
WHO ELSE IN YOUR FAMILY TAKES CARE OF YOU?
My father.
YOUR FATHER . . .
WHAT RESEMBLANCE DO YOU SEE?
You are not very aggressive but I think you don't want me to notice that.
WHAT MAKES YOU THINK I AM NOT VERY AGGRESSIVE?
You don't argue with me.
WHY DO YOU THINK I DON'T ARGUE WITH YOU?
You are afraid of me.
DOES IT PLEASE YOU TO BELIEVE I AM AFRAID OF YOU?
My father is afraid of everybody.
WHAT ELSE COMES TO MIND WHEN YOU THINK OF YOUR FATHER?
Bullies.
DOES THAT HAVE ANYTHING TO DO WITH THE FACT THAT YOUR BOYFRIEND MADE YOU COME HERE?

This conversation, even though laboriously typed out on a teleprinter, is remarkably close to what you might expect from a real live psychologist. It shows how following very simple rules can keep a conversation going, even when one 'end' of the conversation is being conducted by a machine that does not understand the meaning of the utterances; while the two bogus human conversations we quoted earlier break down (or do not properly start) because they break the rules.

We are suggesting that the average person has learnt and

memorised something like a very complicated computer program or book of rules telling him how to choose what to say and do in social and formal conversations. Now we are learning to read exactly what is 'written' in the mental rulebook.

For certain formal occasions such as weddings, funerals, ordinary church services and so on, we have actual rulebooks in the form of prayer books, helped by instructions from the priest. We also have clear sets of rules and expressions—though not always written—for other formal functions such as attendance at courts (please address their Worships), committee meetings (please address the Chairman), parliamentary sessions and so on. Rule-breakers can be penalised for contempt of court, or be ruled out of order.

The how-to-do-it rules for ordinary informal conversation in the pub, social club or corner shop are not as obvious. Victorian ladies used to have manuals on etiquette for everyday situations, which showed them how to conduct themselves properly in every possible situation, from talking to those of higher or lower social rank to receiving the advances of a gentleman or giving orders to a servant.

Rules of etiquette did not die out completely with the Victorians. Some aspects remain with us today, although no longer called etiquette and usually not as elaborate. The greeting, the parting and the apology are three examples.

Rigid etiquette has largely disappeared—but we still conform to some laid-down procedures in greeting and parting.

Erving Goffman describes the greeting as a ritual for two reasons. First, it does not *tell* you anything, but symbolises the beginning of a conversation, in much the same way as a wedding symbolises the start of a marriage. Secondly, as in any ritual, the participants know exactly what they have to do. The following

The handslapping ritual on meeting (adopted by modern urban blacks) is about to begin: each participant knows exactly what to do.

example of a greeting was adapted from a study by Adam Kendon. At an outdoor party of American university staff, cameras recorded guests coming up the long garden drive and being greeted by the host.[3]

The distant salutation
As the guest catches sight of the host some distance away, he waves his arm with the palm of his hand open, 'flashes' his eyebrows (raises and lowers them very quickly), smiles and sometimes tosses his head up and shouts some brief greeting like 'Hi'.

The approach
As the guest approaches the host, he cuts off communication briefly by dipping his head, looking away, bringing an arm across the front of his body and perhaps straightening his tie or stroking his hair. This is all preparation for the close phase.

The close phase
As he comes close to the host, the guest looks up, smiles, offers a handshake and says something like 'Hullo, Barnaby'. He then stops, settles down into a comfortable stance a foot or two away

from the host and asks (or is asked) a conventional question like 'How are you?' By this time, the greeting is more or less over. Without exactly saying so, guest and host have committed themselves to having a brief chat.

Making requests, apologising and saying goodbye are among other polite routines of this kind.

Spontaneous conversation

John and Mike are two acquaintances who meet by chance at the local tavern. Before embarking on a conversation, each sounds the other out. Is he friendly? Is he open for a chat? They don't ask each other this, but use the greeting as the device to do it. If John responds with a smile and a 'How are you?' to Mike's initial greeting, it means they are in business. They have come to an unspoken agreement to spend some time talking and behaving in a special kind of way we call chatting.

Chatting is special, in that it is *not* interviewing, buying and selling, bargaining, teaching or any other kind of conversation, though we wouldn't preclude these other things occurring in a secondary way. It is the most spontaneous of all forms of talk.

Even so, before the conversation has started, decisions and agreements have been made about what John and Mike are going to do together in general terms. This is done not only during the greetings, but also in the opening remarks. Perhaps in his opening remarks John asks Mike what he has been doing recently. If Mike replies appropriately, then the two friends have set the situation up, or as psychologists say, 'negotiated an episode'. This can be seen more clearly in formal situations like committee meetings, where the person in charge asks a member, 'Shall we talk about your proposals now?'

Two people must therefore agree on the definition of the situation, and be prepared to play socially defined parts in it. In the 60s, American hippies, 'acidheads' and teenagers evolved a style known as the 'put-on'. This involved a refusal to accept the appropriate role by adopting deliberately non-meshing responses. Sensible conversation was thus prevented. Here is an example taken from *Playboy* in an interview with the singer Bob Dylan:

PLAYBOY:	How do you get your kicks these days?
DYLAN:	I hire people to look into my eyes, and then I have them kick me.
PLAYBOY:	And that's the way you get your kicks?
DYLAN:	No. Then I forgive them. That's where my kicks come in.
PLAYBOY:	Did you ever have the standard boyhood dream of growing up to be President?
DYLAN:	No. When I was a boy, Harry Truman was President. Who'd want to be Harry Truman?

PLAYBOY: Well, let's suppose that you were the President. What would you accomplish during your first thousand days?

DYLAN: Well, just for laughs, so long as you insist, the first thing I'd do is probably move the White House. Instead of being in Texas it'd be on the East Side of New York. McGeorge Bundy would definitely have to change his name and General McNamara would be forced to wear a coonskin cap and shades.

A conversation between our friends John and Mike is more mundane. Mike describes his recent social activities and John, unlike Dylan, almost certainly and predictably reciprocates with similar experiences. Then John perhaps cracks a joke or tells a funny story about a mutual acquaintance. Mike laughs and is likely to crack a recent joke in reply, or tell a similar funny anecdote. Then to change the subject John and Mike may go on to swap stories about the holidays, problems with the kids, boast about the sizes of vegetables grown or fish caught, each exchanging one experience for a similar one.

This is a simple two-step sequence. A move by John produces a move by Mike, which leads to another by John, and an endless chain of interaction is possible. When they finally want to conclude the conversation, they don't say, 'Shall we stop now?' 'Yes, let's', but they use another familiar and highly-stereotyped social routine, the farewell.

Taking turn and turn about: look for the cues given by each to show willingness to listen rather than talk.

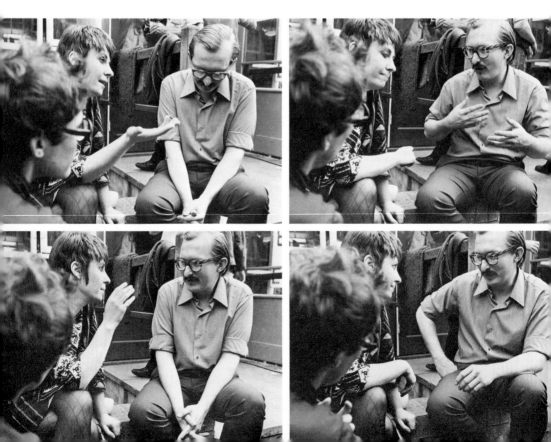

Ending: handshake and a turned body.

It is therefore evident that there are rules for ordinary chat. We have to define the situation, and we negotiate it and agree to abide by it for a length of time. Other rules govern the sort of things we should say in response to each other within that time; for instance, we should ask questions, stick to the topic introduced and so on.

A conversation is usually made up of a number of fairly distinct phases or 'episodes', including a greeting, discussion of various topics, and a conclusion. In more formal encounters, such as church services, dinner parties and committee meetings, these divisions may be quite sharp. In planned sequences conducted by a teacher or interviewer, a series of different episodes are introduced either verbally ('Shall we talk about the work you did in your last job now'), or non-verbally (the teacher rises from the table).

Conversation: the 'sales talk'

There are many familiar situations where *one* participant has it all planned and the other is unprepared. Think of a salesman with a 'prospect'; a Casanova with a naïve girl, a psychotherapist with his patient; and, more formally, a chairman with a committee. All these conversation-planners have a motive or goal in mind: either to sell something, to seduce, to 'cure' or to get decisions made.

Consider one example in some detail—an insurance salesman at work. According to the British consumer magazine *Money Which?*, a life insurance salesman is well-trained in his sales talk.

Setting the situation up

We saw earlier how people use subtle clues to agree on a situation in which they can have a certain kind of interaction. John Juniper does this in an attempt to set up a buying and selling situation. By the 'soft sell' and the implied consent techniques, he tries to tempt Mr Prospect into accepting the situation. Once Mr Prospect has agreed to John Juniper's definition of the situation, John Juniper is halfway to his goal. A Casanova does this with his female prey, as does a psychotherapist with his patient in that he tries to help the patient to see things differently.

Tactics within the situation

In spontaneous conversation, one remark leads to another as each person simply responds to the last comment of the other. This would not do for insurance salesman John Juniper. He is playing a more elaborate game, more akin to chess, and his moves are planned well ahead.

Mr Prospect, caught unawares, does not have a plan, but simply responds to John Juniper's probes. John Juniper selects each probe according to plan and Mr Prospect's last response. He aims to answer any objections and to get straight back to the place he had got to in his script.

The classroom situation differs in that one person is definitely in charge. Ned Flanders, an educational psychologist, noted that good teachers go through various regular cycles of classroom behaviour.[4] One might go like this:

Teacher: Lectures; asks question
Pupils: Answer
Teacher: Develops and clarifies pupils' answers; asks related questions
Pupils: Respond with longer answers, develop line of thought

The teacher skilfully changes tactics to get pupils motivated and involved. Probably unwittingly, he is using two well-known psychological principles. He is using *reinforcement*: he rewards his pupils by appreciating and developing their own ideas. He is also getting *reciprocation*: when the pupils develop ideas and ask questions.

'Two-way' conversations

In conversations such as discussions, bargaining or negotiation sessions, both participants have a plan. Imagine, for instance, if Mr Prospect also has a plan and goal in his meeting with the salesman. Perhaps he wants to get the best possible deal, to turn John Juniper down firmly but politely, or even to teach John Juniper a lesson for his wheeling and dealing. Or suppose Casanova is up against a woman who is out to humiliate him. The sequence of probes and responses will take a very different turn.

When both parties have quite different plans, there may be an argument, followed by one winning or the situation simply breaking up altogether. Alternatively, the participants may be able to negotiate a joint plan. This is possible even when those present are in competition, providing they use their skills and strategies within the rules.

Body and voice in conversation

When we talk, our conscious attention is usually devoted to the words we use. We are usually quite unaware of what we are doing with our bodies or the sounds we are making with our voices. Meanwhile, recent research has shown that this non-verbal communication is not only essential to conversation but adds immeasurably to its richness and versatility. Consider the behaviour of popular talking robots on television, such as the Daleks in the British science fiction series, *Dr Who*. It is not only what they say, but how they say it that creates the weird, inhuman effect—dull, monotonous voices, no facial expression, no gestures, and so on.

Making sense of what we say

Words are often not enough to make sense in conversation, and we use non-verbal ways of getting the message across. When words fail us, gestures often help us out.

Punctuation is an important element in clear message-giving. Written language without punctuation is not easy to follow, as anyone reading *Ulysses* by James Joyce would know. Unpunctuated speech would also be impossible to follow, so we have a non-verbal system for doing the job.

We use short pauses for commas, longer ones for full stops; a rising and falling pitch (or *vice versa*) and raised eyebrows for question marks. We accompany words and phrases with small movements of the hands, face and eyes, sentences with movements of the head or an arm and paragraphs with shifts of the whole body. We use volume and pitch to emphasise words and make meanings clear. For instance, 'They are hunting dogs' could be taken two ways, while 'They are hunting *dogs*' could not.

Finally, having made our statement in all these ways, we can comment on it, to show whether it is meant to be funny, serious, sarcastic. For instance, a complaint or criticism may be accompanied by a wink or smile which completely changes its meaning.

The art of listening

A former British Prime Minister said, 'We must not only govern, but be *seen* to be governing.' This is also true of listening. The good listener doesn't sit motionless, taking it all in, but keeps up a constant flow of mainly non-verbal *attention* signals. If he doesn't, the speaker thinks he isn't listening at all, and will probably stop speaking. Attention signals include sitting in an alert posture, looking often at the speaker, and intermittently nodding, smiling, and making various noises and comments like 'Mhmm', 'Yes', 'Really', 'You don't say?' (American), 'Si, si, si' (Italian).

The good listener also lets the speaker know what he thinks of his statement. Intermittently, and particularly at the end of the speaker's sentence, he smiles or frowns to show whether he likes it or not. He raises his eyebrows to show surprise, or lowers them to show puzzlement, and nods and shakes his head to show agreement and disagreement.

5 Persons and situations

Although it is obvious that we behave differently at parties, funerals, football matches and committee meetings, it is not enough just to say so. We need to describe and classify situations, so that we can say what it is about each of them that produces its characteristic forms of social behaviour.

One way of describing the differences between various kinds of social activity is to say where they fall on these dimensions:

> formal—informal
> work—social
> friendly—unfriendly
> equal—unequal status[1]

Once you ignore the purpose of a situation and concentrate on its more abstract qualities some surprising similarities appear. Joe Forgas found that students rated a wedding and a tutorial as similar, though clearly the behaviour involved is completely different. A study of outdoor games might group together water polo, all-in wrestling and ice hockey, which are similar in their roughness, but which are quite different in other ways.

When we concentrate on the purpose of a situation, we produce a different set of similarities and differences. Each of the standard situations with which we are familiar in a culture, such as meals, seminars and weddings, has its own unique structure which has rules of a different kind from those that make football, ice hockey and table tennis quite different games. Situations involve the following components.

Elements of behaviour

Appropriate social moves at a seminar would include: making long speeches, asking awkward questions, showing slides and writing on the board. These would be completely out of place in most other situations. At meals, dances and dates, for example, gossip or small talk would be more acceptable. Just as every game has special moves, each situation has its repertoire of appropriate behaviour.

Motivation

Each situation, each kind of task, meets a particular need. Sometimes similar needs are met for all present, as in meetings between the sexes or two friends. At other times, the needs are different but complementary, as in buying and selling or teaching and learning. Sometimes a wide range of motivations are involved: a dinner party involves eating, self-presentation, friendship and sitting with the same and the opposite sex.

A garden party pursues a variety of goals in a semi-formal way, calling up particular kinds of behaviour in the guests.

Roles and rules

Every situation has a social structure of its own. A seminar requires a speaker, a chairman, and an audience. Selling involves a salesperson and a customer. Each role carries special duties and demands particular kinds of social behaviour. If you break the rules that apply to a role and a situation, the interaction comes to a stop. This is not just a matter of polite behaviour. If a person

The wrong clothes can disrupt a situation in which people behave according to well-understood rules.

moves his chess pieces as though he were playing draughts or chequers, or tries to play cricket with a football, the game comes to a stop. There is similar disruption when rules intrinsic to a social task are broken: for example, when an interviewee tries to ask all the questions, a mealtime guest refuses to eat, or an audience at a seminar is inattentive. If other rules to do with general self-presentation are broken—if the wrong clothes are worn, for example—these may create discomfort and annoyance, but need not prevent the basic goals of situations from being attained.

Environmental setting

Most situations require special equipment or a special physical setting of some kind. Seminars call for a large room with chairs arranged in a particular way, together with a table, blackboard, and slide-projector, for example. A party needs a quite different kind of room, lighting and furniture, together with food and drink.

Environmental psychologists are concerned primarily with the physical setting of situations. They are interested in facts, such as the distance between people and how the density of various people in a room affects their behaviour. For example, closer distances lead to intimacy, even between strangers, although overcrowding also leads to aggression. Children fight more in an overcrowded play-group. Room temperature is also important. An experiment found that people like each other more if they meet in a room at a comfortable temperature than in one which is much too hot. It is well known that riots are more likely to occur during heat waves.

The visual aspects of situations are also important. If one person can see better than the other, or if the other is better illuminated, the person who can see better is more comfortable, while the other feels uncomfortably self-conscious. This is why interviewers and managers often place their desks so that they sit with their backs to the window. If one person wears dark sunglasses, he is at a considerable advantage because the other is deprived of feedback from the eyes.

The physical aspects of situations also affect social behaviour through their symbolic meanings. For example, if a person is seated in a larger chair, at the head of the table, or at a higher level, he is expected to take charge. Some people arrange their offices with the desk facing the door, so that they dominate the room and their visitors.

The colour of a room affects the mood of those in it. Bright yellow tones are cheerful, red is warm and dark blues are gloomy. Experiments show that we are friendlier towards people when we meet them in an attractively decorated room. The furnishings often suggest the kind of activities for which the room is suitable, be it love, social activity, committee work, or research. It would be difficult to be amorous in a room with a concrete floor, a bare electric light bulb, battered wooden tables and chairs. Such a room would be more appropriate to a prison or interrogation centre.

Research into the effects of situations is a recent development of social psychology with far-reaching implications. If situations are as important as persons in causing a type of behaviour, then perhaps we should put as much effort into dealing with the situations where delinquency arises (like shops, buses, football grounds, areas of high-rise buildings) as we do into delinquent persons. We should treat anxiety-provoking situations (flying, formal occasions, meeting strangers) as intensively as we treat anxious people.

One form of treatment could be situational therapy which is the systematic analysis of problem situations, in order to discover how they might be altered.

*Self-confidence is
grounded in a thorough
understanding of
how to perform
in odd situations.*

People

Different people behave differently in the same situation. Some
are noisy, some nervous, some friendly and others hostile. Many
of these differences are due to personality. In social situations two
personality factors are important, dominant/submissive and
warm/cold. These are quite separate factors, and cross over each
other like this:

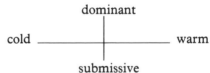

Some people are dominant and cold, others are dominant and
warm. Some are submissive and cold, others are submissive and
warm.

Warm people smile, sit close, and say friendly things.
Dominant people are more assertive, speak louder, air their
opinions, try to influence other people, and like to direct what
happens. Warm people are most concerned with establishing and
maintaining friendly relations: dominant people are more
concerned with the task or topic of conversation, and want to be
in charge of it. Warm people are popular, but it is often the
dominant people who become accepted as leaders.

There are very subtle variations in the way people manifest
this behaviour. Two people may be warm to a similar degree, but
one is warm in facial expression, gaze, posture, and physical
distance, while the other is warm through tone of voice and the
content of speech. Two supervisors may talk as much as each
other, but one asks questions and reacts favourably to suggestions
from the line-workers, while the other just reads sermons and
gives straightforward instructions.

Extroversion and introversion

At the Maudsley Hospital, London, Professor Hans Eysenck has done extensive research which shows that the personalities of these general types of people stem from their physiological make-up. He maintains that extroverts are generally more sociable, more impulsive, prefer stronger stimulation (e.g., loud music) and are slower to learn than introverts.[2] It has been found by others that the *more* extroverted of a pair in conversation was likely to speak first, to talk more and to be more persuasive.

Neurotics are generally prone to high levels of anxiety, low resistance to stress, headaches and other aches and pains, poor sleeping and reduced energy. Neuroticism is also associated with various peculiarities of social behaviour, particularly with anxiety in social situations, tenseness and irritability. All forms of mental disorder lead to failure of one or more aspects of social behaviour. An extreme example is that of paranoia, in which the patient sees the actions of others as part of a planned campaign of hostility against him. Schizophrenia results in basic failures of communication and complete withdrawal from society.

Intelligence and other abilities

When a group is working at some task or discussing a problem, the person who is best at the task is likely to become the leader. If the task changes, so does the leader. In groups of children and students the most intelligent tend to become the leaders—except in gangs of juvenile delinquents, or anti-school cliques, where toughness or ruthlessness may be admired above intelligence.

Just a game—but learning social rules as well.

Attitudes and values

One of the best predictors of whether two people will like one another is the similarity of their attitudes and values. If a group member conforms to the attitudes in a group he will be accepted and perhaps popular. If he holds different views from the group, he is likely to be rejected.

Physical cues

Some of the best cues to predict behaviour are age, sex and social class. These operate in two rather different ways. In the first place, people of different ages are different in themselves in a number of ways. Secondly, they are treated differently, since they occupy different positions in society. The same is true of social class. For example, upper-middle-class people have certain distinguishing characteristics, most of them shared features of their sub-culture, such as the holding of certain beliefs. In addition, they are reacted to in a special way by members of their own and other social classes.

A person's body also affects his or her social behaviour in more than one way. First, there are links between physique and temperament: muscular people have a tendency to be more aggressive, thin people tend to be tense and intellectual. More important than this, however, is the fact that different physiques are reacted to in special ways. In chapter 7 we describe the ways in which attractive girls are treated. Similarly, tall men tend to be selected for leadership positions.

Sex differences in social behaviour are of interest in view of the rise of women's lib. It is hard to say how many of the sex differences in behaviour are innate, and how many are culturally acquired.

However, the male is stronger, more aggressive and more dominant throughout the rest of the animal kingdom. Human males are more concerned with task and achievement, females with interpersonal relations. Females gaze and smile more, are warmer and more expressive, more responsive to situations, and less likely to be socially inadequate.

We have discussed traits, like introversion-extroversion, as they apply universally, to all situations equally. However, some recent research shows that in everyday life we do not see people in this regular scientific way. When we discriminate between each other we use dimensions that are relevant to the immediate situation. Separate groups of people are classed in quite different ways. Thus male students classify girl friends in terms of their attractiveness, talkativeness, self-confidence and intelligence; they classify other male students in terms of introversion-extroversion, radicalism-conservatism, talkativeness and social class.

Persons in situations

*Body-pride: good-looking
people behave more
confidently and boldly
(above) than others.*

We have seen that situations have distinctive rules and roles, and generate distinctive patterns of behaviour. We have also seen that people have stable, underlying properties which lead to somewhat different behaviour in different situations. We shall now put people and situations together, to see how they combine.[3]

Let us take lateness as an example. Suppose that Tom is on average three minutes earlier, and Harry three minutes later than other people and that Dick usually arrives at the same time. And let us suppose that on average people are not late for the doctor, are three minutes late for morning coffee and six minutes late when dining out. Studying Tom, Dick and Harry's lateness might give average lateness as follows:

	doctor	*coffee*	*dinner*	*average*
Tom	3 *mins early*	*on time*	3 *mins late*	0
Dick	*on time*	3 *mins late*	6 *mins late*	3
Harry	3 *mins late*	6 *mins late*	9 *mins late*	6
average	0	3	6	

Here each individual's deviation from normal is simply added to the situation's typical lateness. The situation might be more important than the person, as in the following example, where the situations have twice as much effect as the persons:

	dentist	*coffee*	*party*	*average*
Tom	−6	0	6	0
Dick	−3	3	9	3
Harry	0	6	12	6
average	−3	3	9	

However what is found is usually different, because different people respond in special ways to particular situations. Harry, for example, is frightened of the dentist and gets there later, but is very keen on parties and gets there earlier, than the combination of averages would predict. Tom does not mind the dentist but hates parties:

	dentist	*coffee*	*party*	*average*
Tom	−11	0	+11	0
Dick	−3	3	9	3
Harry	5	6	7	6
average	−3	3	9	

The average lateness for each person and each situation are exactly the same as before, but they are made up in different ways.

Now consider difficulty and anxiety in different situations. We can rate how anxious we feel on a 5-point scale:

1	2	3	4	5
no anxiety	slight anxiety	moderate anxiety	great anxiety	avoidance

Suppose your average score for many social situations is 2, which means that on average you feel slightly anxious. We know the average scores for anxiety in many of these situations. In one study of students we found the following percentages, with an average score of 2 or more:

Situation	*People scoring 2 or more* (per cent)
going to dances, discos	35
going out with opposite sex	21
meeting strangers	13
entertaining in home	7
being with close friends	1

Each of us has a characteristic anxiety pattern. For example, some people are upset by parties, some by appearing in public, others by intimate situations with the opposite sex. There are, of course, some people who feel anxious in nearly all social situations, as well as those who are anxious in none but they are rather rare. So although people have some degree of consistency across situations, they are inconsistent because varying situations bring out different behaviour in everyone.

We now know that some individuals are more consistent than others. Rather surprisingly, mental patients are *more* consistent than normal people. As they get better their behaviour comes to vary more between situations. Their behaviour becomes less rigid and stereotyped, more responsive to the demands of situations. Women are less consistent than men—perhaps confirming the ancient tradition that women are fickle. Japanese people appear more affected by situations than Westerners, as a result of the elaborate rules of etiquette governing proper behaviour in situations, like the tea ceremony with its intricate rules for the making and serving of tea.

There is an interesting dimension of personality that distinguishes between those who are more and less consistent. This is known as *internal–external control.* Internal controllers think that what will happen in a situation is under their own control, while external controllers think that what will happen depends on other people or on chance. Internal controllers are less affected by conformity and other social pressures, are more curious, ask more questions, and make longer-term plans.

However, there are further factors about the ways in which persons and situations combine. People usually enter situations because they choose to do so. Indeed, a useful way of assessing people is to determine the situations they like and those they avoid. So personality affects the situation which is chosen as well as the behaviour once it has been entered. Secondly, people modify situations to some extent, once they are in them. They may actually renegotiate the situation, turning a party into a kind of seminar, or *vice versa.* Or they may create a characteristic mood, or social atmosphere, of gloom, or jollity, wherever they go. Some elicit characteristic reactions from all they meet, so that they are constantly surrounded by people who appear to be very shy, very friendly or very bad-tempered. These may be experienced as objective features of situation, but are actually generated by the person himself.

6   Sense of self

'Who am I?' The self is used in two main senses in psychology: the 'me' and the 'I'. The self-image, or the 'me', comprises our thoughts and feelings about ourselves. For just as we form impressions of others, we also form impressions of ourselves. We take a look at ourselves from the outside, as we imagine others see us. This is quite different from the second sense, the 'I', the conscious subject, that does the seeing and decision-taking.

The 'me' consists of two parts. The *self-image* is the descriptive part—the sort of person we think we are. *Self-esteem* is a measure of how favourably we regard ourselves. When we are in front of audiences, mirrors or TV cameras, the 'me' becomes prominent. In conversation, our focus of attention shifts from the 'I' to the 'me' as we take our point of view or that of others. The self-image is not always fully conscious, or expressed in words.

A person might rate herself as fairly fat (self-image), but would like to be fairly thin (ideal image), and would mark such a scale as follows:

	ideal self			self-image	
thin	X			X	fat

She would have a conflict score of four points for this particular scale, which is very high.

Another aspect of the self is the extent to which a person has achieved some degree of integration of his various ambitions, interests and activities. The psychoanalyst Erik Erikson[1] proposed four degrees of integration:

1. Basic decisions about occupation, marriage and values have been taken.
2. These decisions have been postponed, e.g., while at college.
3. Decisions have been taken early, but while in a dependent rather than a mature state.
4. No decisions have been taken, no commitment to career or other goals.

*Trying out 'me' for size:
it is 'I' who watches,
'me' who is watched.*

Other common states of the identity have been observed by other investigators. There is the 'contented drop-out' syndrome, and there is the person who cannot decide between two alternative sets of goals; for example, between possible careers, or between work and politics. An example of the second is a young man who couldn't decide whether to be a clergyman or a whisky distiller, and was thinking of solving his problem by going into the manufacture of sacramental wine.

If you ask someone to answer the question, 'Who am I?' twenty times, you will find that the answers are of two main kinds; *roles*, e.g., age, sex, occupation, family relationships, religion; and *personality traits* and *evaluations*, e.g., happy, good, intelligent. Peter White, at Oxford, had used an even more open-ended method; he simply asked people to write about themselves for an hour. Older people were found to write a lot about their past life, while younger people wrote about their immediate concerns.

Another aspect of the self is the *body-image*, of which the most important aspects are its perceived size and attractiveness.

Individuals also differ in their self-consciousness. Argyle and Marylin Williams explored the conditions under which people feel self-conscious. They found that while some people feel as though they are observers in social situations, others were self-conscious and felt as though they were observed. These people are attending mainly to 'me' rather than 'I'. Their self-image is unduly prominent, but not consistent, and they are low in self-esteem. Not surprisingly an interviewer is more likely to feel himself an observer than an interviewer. But if an older person is talking to a younger the older one is more likely to feel like an observer and the younger as though he were being observed. Similarly, in our society males more often feel like observers and females more often feel under observation.

How 'I' and 'me' are assigned: men in our society see themselves as observers, women as the observed.

How the self-image is acquired

The reactions of others

The most important source of the self-image is probably the reactions of others. We discover how others see us and we partly accept their view of us. This is the 'looking-glass' theory of the self—to see ourselves we look to see how we are reflected in the reactions of others. If parents tell a child that he is clever, or treat him as if he is untrustworthy, he may come to believe it. These attributes may thus become part of his self-image.

Mother's disciplining finger is an important pointer, for the child, to the delineation of his self-image.

Children receive a lot of fairly direct information about how others see them. Among adults, however, there is something of a taboo on direct verbal comments, especially negative ones. Nevertheless, non-verbal messages are not without impact. A smile or grimace from Jack, for example, is enough to tell Jill what he thinks of her appearance or something she has said. The more mature we are and the more integrated our self-image, the less effect non-verbal messages have on the self-image—except perhaps when the reactions come from someone whose views are greatly respected. It is the reactions of others that keep our self-image fairly close to reality; and there are powerful forces pulling it away from reality, as we shall see. Feelings of inferiority—that is low self-esteem—are not due to a person really being inferior, but either to disparaging reactions from parents and teachers in childhood, or because he has chosen too superior a group to compare himself with.

Make-believe—but also trying to catch the virtue of an admired model (above) or pre-testing an adult social custom such as a wedding (below).

Comparison with others

Most self-perceptions are based on comparison. Fred, for example, is taller than John and that makes John feel short. If a child's brothers and sisters are dimmer than he is, he will come to regard himself as clever however bright he really is. If the other children at school come from richer homes he will come to regard his family as poor. Experiments have shown that people are eager to evaluate themselves, and that they do so by comparing their performance, say at tennis, with those who are of a similar standard or slightly above, but not with Wimbledon champions or hopeless beginners.

Roles played

Roles and occupations are an important part of the self-image. Adults often see themselves primarily in terms of occupational roles, unless they have performed other roles of greater prestige or involvement. Medical students as they go through their training gradually come to see themselves as 'doctors'. When someone first plays a role, he feels he is acting a part. But when he has played it for some time and others have accepted him in this role, it becomes part of his self-image and is no longer a mask.

Identifying with models

As children grow up they adopt a series of other people as models with whom to identify—parents, older children, teachers, film stars and so on. The *ideal* self is mainly based on these models, though a person is not chosen as a model unless he exemplifies ideals already embraced. Research has shown, however, that the self-image as well as the ideal self is affected. A person feels that he already shares some of the attributes of the model. In this way an important part of the self is acquired.

Adolescent identity-formation

Much of children's play consists of enacting adult roles. Adolescents try out these roles more seriously; during student life it is possible to experiment with a number of roles and

identities without much commitment. However, between the ages of 16 and 24 there are increasing pressures on young people to decide which of their bits and pieces of identity they are going to take seriously, and which will be suppressed. These pressures are partly due to the need to make a number of important decisions—about education, occupation, spouse and general life-style. The adolescent also has growing powers of abstract thinking. He becomes particularly concerned about the consistency of his behaviour: for example, being consistently honest, radical, vegetarian or whatever.

This effort to achieve an integrated self-image during adolescence gives rise to what Erikson described as an 'identity crisis', and to the various stages in identity-formation mentioned

Trying to fix the fluid identity of adolescence can bring bizarre results.

earlier. The formation of an identity is made easier by the existence of a number of familiar social types in the community offering ready-made identities. An English girl might consider becoming a secretary, schoolteacher or a fashion model, but probably not a priestess or an elephant trainer. The chosen identity, however, is likely to be an individualised version of a social type, such as an *intellectual* model, as opposed to just a pretty face.

Adolescents have the further problem of establishing an identity that is somewhat independent of the family, though it usually has much in common with it. This is usually achieved by joining a social group outside the family and accepting its values; for example, a group which is more religious, more intellectual, or more delinquent than the family.

Forces affecting self-image

There are powerful forces that push and pull the self-image. According to one theory, our main drive is towards consistency: that is, we seek reactions from others that are consistent with how we see ourselves. We want to be admired for whatever we admire in ourselves. The American psychologist Carl Rogers, however, maintains that we are primarily concerned with maximising self-esteem; in other words, we seek a favourable self-image and favourable reactions from others.

A number of experiments have pitted the two theories against each other. For example, subjects were praised when they had done badly (which satisfies self-esteem but not consistency). It was found that such unwarranted praise was not believed or remembered, but the evaluation was liked and self-esteem was enhanced—proving that both processes work, in different ways. Self-esteem seems to be particularly important in the Far East, where loss of face is a major disaster, and may lead to suicide.

The effect of making people self-conscious

Shelly Duval and Robert Wickland used mirrors and TV cameras to find out what happens when we become aware of a discrepancy between our self-image and the view of others, or between our self-image and actual behaviour; for example, a fat person who had formed the somewhat inaccurate picture of herself as thin. They found that either we run away from the truth or we face up to it and change our ideas. When the people in their experiment were aware of the difference between their ideas about themselves and the facts in the mirror, they would spend less time examining their image than others. When they were actually in front of the mirror they gave more honest replies to questionnaires and less favourable self-ratings.[2]

Preserving the self-image

As a result of the motivations described, most people's self-image is rather more favourable and more consistent than is really justified. There is some danger that it will be damaged by the reactions of others, who are not so motivated to preserve our self-image. The American psychologists Paul Secord and Carl Backman have pointed out several ways in which we deal with this danger:

1. Mixing only with those who share our view of ourself, such as our immediate circle of friends.
2. Changing group membership, to a comparison group of lower performance or status, such as a less prestigious club, or a tennis club of poorer players.
3. Actually changing behaviour, so as to make the reactions

of others more favourable; conforming to group norms is one way.

4. Forming a lower opinion of those who do not share our self-image—as when a child rejects a teacher who gives him low marks.

5. Ignoring or disbelieving what they say—as when a scientist ignores the reactions of other scientists about his work and presses on regardless.

Galileo's strong self-image allowed him to ignore scepticism and pursue his theories.

Developing the self-image

The self-image is not static, but is being forever pulled upwards by the ideal self. A high jumper who knows he can jump 1·9 metres (self-image) would like to be able to reach two metres (ideal self). When he has done so, he revises both his self-image and his ideal self, setting himself higher goals and perhaps choosing different models to identify with. Abraham Maslow has suggested that we have a motivation to grow, develop and improve, though this may be a reflection of the achievement drives which are a typically Western characteristic. Carl Backman suggests that we try out with friends new developments in the self-image: if they accept it, this part of the self is more firmly established. A similar process occurs in social-skills training, when new styles of social behaviour are tried out first in the laboratory or clinic.

Jean-Paul Sartre argued that we create our personalities in much the same way that writers create their characters. George Bernard Shaw and George Orwell appear to have created new characters for themselves, in a heightened version of this process. Shaw rejected his early identity as a clerk and built up a more exciting one—the left-wing pamphleteer and dramatist. George Orwell not only created a new identity for himself, but a new name as well.

Self-presentation

Dressing for the part: 'Look, I'm a student'.

Identifying oneself as (left) a group member and (right) as holding certain beliefs.

'Self-presentation' is behaviour designed to create an impression for others. As we have seen, we are strongly motivated to produce such impressions; in particular to get favourable reactions which will confirm our self-image and self-esteem. These needs are particularly strong in those uncertain of their self-image. In *The Presentation of Self in Everyday Life* Erving Goffman argued that this often has to be inferred from clothes and other visible features. These can easily be manipulated to give a good impression, and much deliberate deception takes place. This 'impression management' is like behaviour on stage. For example, members of the family combine to put on a good show for the guests, who are allowed to see only the more presentable parts of the house.[3]

This theory best fits undertakers, salesmen, waiters and other professional performers who are in the public eye. Other aspects of everyday life may be like a stage in some ways; we are often aware of playing to an audience, and some of the performances become rather standardised. On the other hand, the part we play is our own personality rather than one written by a playwright. We therefore have to improvise a great deal.

Embarrassment

According to Goffman's theory, embarrassment is caused by the exposure of false self-presentation. Edward Gross and Gregor Stone collected from students nearly 1,000 instances of embarrassment. Those that fitted in with the Goffman theory included making mistakes in public, exposure of a phoney front and invasion of back regions, such as the shabbier staff quarters of a public building. Many, however, did not accord with the theory—social gaffes and accidents such as forgetting names and rule-breaking of a variety of kinds.

Embarrassment seems to be a form of social anxiety which can be brought about in different ways. It can be avoided to some extent by accurate or honest self-presentation, and by possession of sufficient social skill. Others avoid embarrassment by making a joke of it.

In another society the public backside scratcher might cause, and suffer, embarrassment.

Deception and concealment

Goffman maintained that deception is common, but his evidence was drawn mainly from waiters and other special professions. Mild degrees of exaggeration and self-enhancement are probably common as part of the process of moving towards the ideal self, but major deception is much rarer.

Concealment, on the other hand, is widespread. We do not tell everyone about our weak points or the most discreditable episodes in our past life, and they in turn collaborate by avoiding reference to them. Major concealment and some deception are practised by those who are stigmatised: homosexuals, alcoholics, drug-addicts, ex-convicts, not to mention secret agents.

Sidney Jourard of the University of Florida found that people disclose most about themselves to mothers, same-sex friends and

73

spouses, and that women give and receive more personal information than men. He also showed that the more one person discloses, the more the other will disclose. Jourard maintained that frankness and self-disclosure make for good mental health. It could, however, be argued that some kinds of concealment are desirable—for example, inappropriate loves and hates.

Verbal self-presentation

Boasting is the simplest and most direct means of self-presentation. In Western culture, this is not generally acceptable, and often results in incredulity and mirth. American psychologists Edward Jones and Kenneth Gergen carried out experiments in which subjects were asked to make themselves attractive to someone else for various purposes. It was found that they did this strategically, with considerable modesty if they were of higher status, and they described their good points in unimportant areas if they were of lower status.

The English writer Stephen Potter, author of *Lifemanship* and other books, has drawn attention to the ways in which people can make themselves look ridiculous by name-dropping: 'As I was saying to the Prime Minister', and so on.

There are, however, situational differences in the operation of this taboo. Applicants for jobs are allowed to describe their successes—though due modesty is expected here too. In encounter groups, members are sometimes asked to tell each other the most important things about themselves.

Saying it without words

The wearing of beads is enough to proclaim a whole way of life.

Self-presentation is done largely by means of non-verbal communication: clothes, hair and other aspects of appearance, accent and speech style, and the overall manner of verbal and non-verbal performance.

Clothes

Keith Gibbins found a high level of agreement among girls about the kind of girls who would wear certain kinds of boots, skirts and other items of clothing. They agreed on whether they would be snobbish, fun-loving, rebellious, shy, gay, promiscuous, and whether they would smoke or drink. Clothes can clearly convey quite detailed information, especially badges or outfits associated with particular social groups, and by how tidy, brightly-coloured and expensive they are.

Hair, skin and physique

The hair is another important area, for both sexes. The length of male hair has been an important signal in recent years. One theory is that long hair is worn by outcasts, wild animals and those beyond social control, though in recent years its meaning has obviously changed; another is that cutting the hair symbolises castration, which might explain the intense resistance often felt towards cutting off long hair. The skin is tattooed or otherwise decorated in some cultures; the removal of tattooing and scars has been found to help towards rehabilitating criminals. The body is often bound or padded by women to approximate to a more fashionable shape.

Status

This is one of the main aims of self-preservtion by appearance. The pursuit of status is probably an explanation for the constant change of fashions. When *élite* fashions are copied by those of lower status, the upper-status groups adopt new fashions to show their distinctiveness. This was shown in a comprehensive study published in 1929 by E. B. Hurlock. He found that 49 per cent of women and 20 per cent of men would follow a fashion in order to appear equal to their social superiors, and about 50 per cent said they dropped a style when their social inferiors adopted it.[4]

Another important indicator of social class, especially in Britain, is speech accent. There are regional as well as class differences, which complicates the issue. Another problem is that a person is often able to speak in a range of accents, usually accommodating to some extent to the company he is in. Except in the case of trained actors, a false upper-class accent, however, is readily detectable.

Physical attractiveness

Physical attractiveness can be manipulated to a large degree by attention to face, hair, physique and clothes. Indeed, it can be regarded as a kind of deliberate behaviour rather than an innate property of the person, and the surprising thing is that so many women (and men) fail to make use of it in order to realise the benefits which follow. As we shall see later, increased attractiveness is being used successfully in sex therapy.

Rebels

Rebels consider themselves to be different from other people in society, and often alter their physical appearance to declare their deviance. At the height of the hippie movement its members did not just wear simple clothes but dressed in a particular style that made them instantly recognisable. The punk rock craze has taken deviance even further, at least in a courageous few.

Inside deviant groups variations that the rest of us would not notice show different classes of membership of the group. In Britain football 'hooligans' have adopted a uniform of long scarves in team colours, often tied round the arm rather than worn round the neck, and trousers, boots, and jackets of a particular style. Inside this group are several sub-groups: boys who have just joined, older boys who are about to leave, 'hooligans' and 'nutters'. Each wears a variation of the basic uniform that is recognisable to the others in the group. At the same time as these 'deviants' signal their difference from the rest of society they indicate solidarity—but with status differences like the rest of society.

7 Friendship and love

Making friends and finding a marriage partner are two of the most important things we do in our lives, yet they are probably the most difficult. Bridget Bryant, Peter Trower and their colleagues in Oxford, England, asked more than 200 students to select the most difficult of 30 social activities. A large number picked going out with someone of the opposite sex and making friends. We asked nearly 100 psychiatric outpatients the same questions and the response was much the same, except that they found the difficulty even higher, and had less success. Male patients had the most trouble and felt inadequate in both spheres. A large number of the men—40 per cent—had failed to find a partner, some having never been out with a girl. Most had few or no friends.

How do people make friends? How does a love relationship develop? What goes wrong for the lonely people? In this chapter we try to piece together the known facts about love and friendship and make some guesses about why it sometimes does not work.

Friendship

What is it about certain people that attracts us to them, makes us want to know them better, perhaps even to become close friends with them? A number of studies have now been done that help us to unravel many of the influences that help friendship to form.[1]

Physical attraction

Physical appearance obviously plays a big role in attracting sexual partners to each other. But does it affect the choice of friends where there is no sexual element (at least not overt)? The answer is yes, physical appearance strongly influences friendship selection.

Although the power of beauty has been known for centuries, the extent of this power has only been discovered quite recently. A number of scientific studies seem to demonstrate that beauty is not skin-deep, in the eye of the beholder. Although we may baulk at the idea, it appears that most of us think that what looks good on the outside must be good inside too. Physically attractive people are believed to possess all sorts of positive qualities, such

*One of the most
difficult
and important things
we ever do—finding
someone to love
who will love us too.*

as being sensitive, kind, interesting, strong and sociable. The behaviour of people in many different settings, from dance floors to court rooms, has shown that we like and trust the physically attractive more than the unattractive—at least on first acquaintance. Although we may intend to judge a person on the basis of his or her personal qualities, they are not visible at first sight. In our ignorance, we tend to deduce them from the most obvious physical attributes.

So attractiveness is important in friendship, not only for its own sake but because we want to select a friend whom we believe to possess all the positive qualities that attractiveness implies.

Individuals differ in what they find attractive in others, and there are cultural and fashionable variations too. Nevertheless some psychologists have successfully isolated some aspects of appearance that seem attractive or repulsive to the majority of people. Apart from facial beauty, positive features include certain kinds of dress, body-build, tallness and beards in men, and expressive behaviours such as smiling. Fatness on the other hand is a negative characteristic in our culture.

'Beauty' is so important in finding friends or lovers that people all over the world will endure great discomfort to gain it.

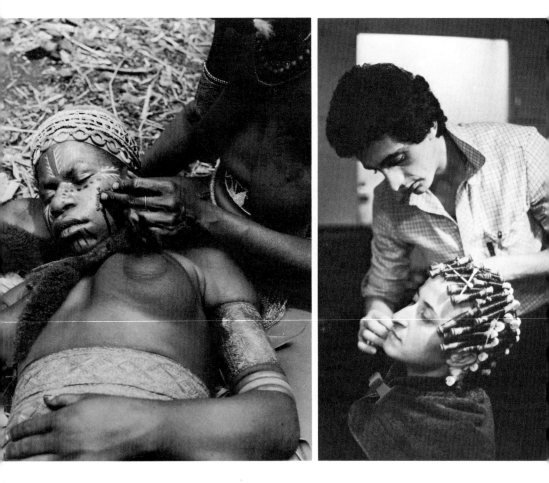

Fashionable and smart clothes are associated with good qualities, and well-dressed people have been found to get more information and cooperation from complete strangers. A woman was given more offers of help with her broken-down car when she dressed attractively than when she dressed less appealingly.

Body-build is another important appearance cue. One study found that even five-year-old children thought that people with a medium muscular build were 'better' than those who were either fat or thin. Tall people are thought to possess stature in other ways. In 1971 sociologist S. D. Feldman noted that every American president elected since 1900 has been the taller of the two major candidates. The *Wall Street Journal* notes that taller graduates got starting salaries averaging 12 per cent higher than their shorter rivals.

Do good-looking people really possess such favourable qualities? Or to put it another way, is beauty really more than skin-deep? Probably yes, at least sometimes. If attractive people are seen positively, they will usually be treated well and so will have more rewarding experiences, will be involved in more social groups and have more potential for friendships than people seen as physically unattractive. This in turn could increase their confidence and make them more rewarding to others. It has been shown that physically attractive people were rated as more socially skilled over the telephone, when their looks are invisible.

The American psychologist Robert Rosenthal found that when teachers believe that a child is more, or less, intelligent than his class-mates then that child will do better, or worse, in class whatever his real ability. Rosenthal called this the Pygmalion Effect. He reports the effect operating to a surprising degree in schools, offices and factories. Teachers and supervisors often have a first-impression prejudice, for instance that black, poor or unattractive children and workers will do worse than others because they are less capable. Not surprisingly, these groups in fact do worse, but often, it seems, because of the way these same teachers and supervisors treat them. For instance, they may be colder towards them, make negative comments, and give them less challenging work and opportunity. Rosenthal describes this as a self-fulfilling prophecy: people do worse, or better, simply because they are expected to and are treated accordingly.

It seems likely, then, that if two people like each other initially because of their looks, they are likely to be nice to each other and for *that* reason become friends. This may explain the results of a study carried out at a boys' summer camp. New arrivals were shown head-and-shoulder photographs of boys in the camp, and asked which ones they would like to have as playmates. Nearly 64 per cent of the boys chose, unknown to them, the most popular boys in the camp. Physical appearance is an important determinant of a playmate's likeability, even for young boys.

Contact

A person may be the most stunning individual who ever walked, yet unless he actually comes into contact with other people, he will have few friends. The more contact we have with someone over a period of time, the more we feel attracted to them (as long as our initial response was not one of repulsion). This contact is accidental and not by choice. Students who share a dormitory or apartment, or who sit near each other in class, will become friends just because of this chance closeness. Clerks in a large department store and members of a bomber crew developed closer relations with those who happened to work next to them than with co-workers a few feet away.

Leon Festinger and colleagues suggested that architects may determine the social life of residents simply by the design of buildings—the way rooms are located on a floor, the way a central staircase is placed in a block of flats, the pavement arrangements on a housing estate and the distance between flats and houses.

Every modern comfort— but will an ancient one, the closeness of family, be promoted by it?

Similarity of attitudes

Neither good looks nor contact will help much if two people are always quarrelling, so similarity of attitudes would seem to be essential to friendship.[2] For example, a group of college students living together, who had not known each other before, were studied over the course of 16 weeks, in order to see who became friendly with whom. Ted Newcomb, the psychologist who reported this study, found that people with similar attitudes tended to choose each other, although this took some time.

Newcomb's study certainly shows that this process takes

place. In addition, however, there is extensive evidence for the process of conformity, whereby people agree with the majority opinion in a group. To begin with they pretend to agree, but later on internalisation takes place and they have really changed their minds.

People are more attracted to each other if they agree on important rather than trivial things. And although people do not have to agree about everything to be friends, the more things they agree about the friendlier they will be.

Apart from similar attitudes, do people have to have similar personalities to be mutually attracted? On the whole the evidence suggests that it does not really matter. Two introverts will not necessarily get on better than an introvert and an extrovert.

Should people be similar in other ways? It helps if they are of similar intelligence, come from a similar social class and background and have similar interests and experiences.

Why does similarity lead to friendship? It enables people to share things to talk about and do together, and to help one another in a cooperative relationship. Similarity of attitudes also lends social support for each other's view of the world. Think of the effect of someone disagreeing with an opinion you hold strongly. It suggests the possibility that you may be wrong and can lead to embarrassment if you feel you have made a fool of yourself in expressing a point of view.

When two people are attracted to each other, see a lot of each other and are similar in attitude and other ways, the chances of friendship are very high. Unfortunately, these three influences do not always combine so conveniently. Suppose John and Steve like each other but disagree violently about religion. Rather than break the friendship up, they may dismiss religion as an irrelevant topic, or one of them may distort the extent of the other's aversion to religion. In one study of married couples each spouse thought the other held almost identical political views. In fact the political attitudes of each couple were almost completely different.

The need to see others as agreeing with us can lead us to attribute all sorts of positive qualities to people who in *fact* agree with us. When subjects were asked to evaluate a stranger with whom they agreed, he was rated as intelligent, knowledgeable about current events, moral and well-adjusted; a disagreeing stranger was evaluated negatively on each of these characteristics.

Attitude-similarity may even influence such objective judgements as estimates of height, disliked people being seen as shorter than liked ones. President Lyndon Johnson's height was estimated as greater by those who liked him than by those who didn't.

In the early stages there are things apart from appearance and similarity that determine attraction. For one thing, the timing may not be right. You may be depressed, it may be too hot or too cold, you may be hungry or in pain, or even have your hair in curlers.

C. Gouaux made his subjects depressed or elated by showing them sad or happy films. They were then told about various strangers who had few, some, or many attitudes in common with their own. At all three levels the 'elated' subjects reacted more favourably towards the strangers.

The effects of physical comfort have similar effects. The more people are made to feel uncomfortable by extremes of temperature and humidity, the more negative their responses are found to be towards others. Abraham Maslow suggested we have a hierarchy of needs, with man's more basic needs, such as survival, at the bottom of an imaginary tree. Unless these needs are satisfied he is unable to seek less basic satisfaction.

The stages of friendship

First stage

Suppose you are at a small party where you find yourself in a corner with your host, Joe, and an attractive girl you've never met.

Joe introduces you to the girl, then says as he starts to walk away, 'Will you excuse me. I'm going to put on some records.' You and the girl look at each other in awkward silence. You feel it's up to you to speak. American psychologist Jean Goldsmith asked a group of people which of the following they would say:

- (a) 'Hello.'
- (b) 'Gee, here we are looking at each other in awkward silence.'
- (c) 'I get the feeling Joe has set you and me up.'
- (d) 'Let's sit down and talk.'

You manage to start the conversation. Now she says: 'Tell me about yourself.' How do you go on?

- (a) 'I like attractive women, the type you have a permanent friendship with.'
- (b) 'I'm really not very interesting.'
- (c) 'You first!'
- (d) 'Is there anything in particular you would like to know about me? I could tell you about what I do for a start.'

As the conversation progresses, you get the feeling the girl is not interested in you as she keeps looking around the room. Now you ask her about a certain TV programme, but she doesn't answer. You realise that she has not even been listening. What do you say?

- (a) 'What are you thinking about?'
- (b) 'Excuse me, I have to go to the bathroom.'
- (c) 'I think I'll get another drink. Would you like to come with me?'

The last answer in each case was judged to be the most competent.

These examples show some of the difficulties present in a first encounter. The couple know little or nothing about each other so they have little to talk about. They are fearful of putting a foot in it, yet do not want to be committed in case they do not much like each other.

For these reasons, we usually begin our encounters with 'safe', rather formal, social routines, such as the greeting and the introduction. Here are some common routines used in approaches to complete strangers in England, in a place like a pub or a station waiting-room:

'Nice day.'   (*conventional aside*)

'Have you got a light?'   (*asking a favour*)

'Busy tonight.'   (*comment about the situation*)

When people have met once or twice before, but are still comparative strangers, the routine is slightly different. Here is an American example, given by the psychiatrist Eric Berne:

'Hi.'

'Hi.'

'Warm enough for you?'

'Sure is. Looks like rain though.'

Conversations about the weather, or similar vacuous topics, can be kept going for quite a long time. No information is exchanged at a verbal level, but the opportunity is created for non-verbal signals to be exchanged. There are cultural conventions about how long these initial moves should last; for old-fashioned Arab chiefs three days was the prescribed period. At some point, the conversation either stops or moves on to a different level and 'exchange of identities' in which each tells 'who' they are:

'I've just moved to this area.'

'I work at . . . '

During this period the two people let each other know whether they want to continue the relationship. This is usually done at a non-verbal level—that is, not 'I rather like you, let's be friends' but rather by smiles, vocal intonation, gaze and body-orientation.

Another thing that new acquaintances do at this early stage is to present themselves in a favourable light. This is usually done with due 'modesty'. For instance, boasting is done by nuance, in the form of an aside rather than a bald statement: 'My son, who is a medical student, tells me that . . . '.

Second stage

Later stages of friendship blend into early stages of love.

By the second stage, the would-be friends have decided they basically like each other. They now need to explore the ground further, particularly about mutual attitudes and feelings. The

partners start disclosing more, for instance about things that worry or anger them, about their parents or spouses, about their problems, weaknesses and so on.

In one experiment, British psychologist John Davis got pairs of strangers to meet regularly over a period of weeks. He found that they talked about increasingly intimate things, that they matched each other's intimacy level, and the more disclosing partner led the way while the more reticent one followed. In mixed couples Davis found that the men usually set the pace, even when they did not make the opening move. Perhaps surprisingly, the men in his study also revealed more intimate things about themselves than the women.

Sociologists Marvin Scott and Stanford Lyman report that the style of interaction becomes more casual at this stage. As more background information is shared, so there is less elaboration of facts and more use of slang and jargon. The partners also make plans to do things together, lend and borrow each other's things and help each other in other ways. There are non-verbal changes: they sit and stand closer together, usually side by side; they probably look and touch more, adopt relaxed postures and mesh their conversation more smoothly.

Sexual attraction

We have seen the power of attractiveness cues in friendship. When love and sex become the focus of the relationship, a specialised set of signals comes into operation. In his book *Intimate Behaviour* Desmond Morris[3] has outlined a number of sexual signals designed mainly to bring about sexual contact, this contact being a first step in the growth of love.

Feminine sex signals
Women have a far more elaborate and important repertoire of sex signals than men, probably because in most cultures the women do the attracting, while the men do the pursuing. The celebrated differences between male and female anatomies point to the most obvious body cues of feminine sexuality: the breasts, buttocks, legs, hips and waist, as well as differences in skin texture, face shape and hair. The genital areas are usually covered by clothes, but Morris suggests there are genital 'echoes' such as breasts for buttocks, lips for genitalia, and that women emphasise

Sealed with a kiss ... or a genital symbol to enhance a come-on?

the similarities by use of special bras and lipsticks. There is, however, no evidence to prove this theory. As well as body signals there are behavioural ones, such as special gestures, postures and patterns of gaze mentioned earlier.

What do men look for in women?

Andrew Mathews, working in Oxford, showed a group of men some pictures of women ranging from the fully-clothed to others who were completely naked. There was a fair amount of agreement as to which women were the most sexually desirable. The most desirable women were described as attractive, sexually inviting, graceful, young and slender. But beyond this agreement some personality differences were also observed.

There is a popularly held belief that men can be classified into three groups, according to the part of the female body they like most: 'breast men', 'buttock men', and 'leg men'. Jerry Wiggins and his colleagues at the University of Illinois asked a group of students to rate nude female silhouettes, saying which part of the body they preferred. The results confirmed the popular belief, in that the men could be divided into three groups. It was also found that different groups of men not only preferred different female forms, but also had different personalities, outlooks and interests.

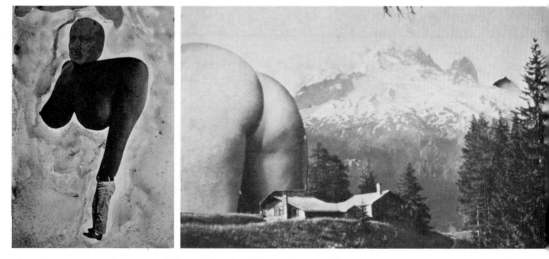

A man of parts—and the parts he fixes on.

Men who liked large-breasted women tended to be *Playboy* readers, smokers, sportsmen, being extrovert and 'masculine' in their interests, whereas the men who preferred fully clothed small-breasted women were introverts, submissive, drank little alcohol and held fundamentalist religious beliefs. Mathews suggests that introverted men are more likely to feel overwhelmed by naked, well-developed women and feel more at ease with the thin and thoughtful-looking.

Men who liked large buttocks were characterised by a need for order and neatness. Those preferring small buttocks were deeply involved in their work and interested in sport.

Of the 'leg men', the sociable extroverts preferred women with small legs, as opposed to the non-drinking submissive male who was more attracted to females with large legs.

The study also suggested that ambitious and heavy-drinking men preferred large women, whereas those who preferred smaller women tended to be more persevering, less sociable, submissive and religious.

There is evidence to suggest that social class also plays an important part in what a man finds attractive in a woman. A group of men comprised of psychiatrists, psychologists, college porters, maintenance men and soldiers, were shown 50 photographs of women, one-third fully dressed, one-third in bikinis and the rest naked. The men were asked to express their opinion of the girls as a marriage partner, and as a short-term sexual partner.

Some of the women appealed to all the men, but there was a tendency for the porters and soldiers to prefer photos of large-breasted nudes. The psychologists on the other hand liked young, well-covered girls, who were displaying arms and legs and who were unconventional or provocative. When nominating possible wives, all the men tended to chose attractive and conventionally dressed women, avoiding sexy and provocative poses.

There is a destiny that shapes our ends—and it sometimes does it well!

So, what a man finds attractive in a woman will depend, above and beyond the cultural norm, on his personality, his social class and what he wants the woman for.

What do women look for in men?

No, not every girl's beau ideal: *something taller—and smaller— is what is wanted.*

A poll conducted by a New York newspaper, *Village Voice*, went some way to dispelling the popular idea that women most admire a muscular chest and shoulders and a large penis, especially when accentuated in tight trousers. Apparently the women preferred men with small buttocks, followed by preferences for tallness and slimness.

However, the true picture is slightly more complicated. When Andrew Mathews and colleagues repeated the experiment in England, this time with women rating photographs of men in various states of dress and undress, they found a large social class difference. Nurses and cleaning staff preferred muscular men, whereas professional women found them repulsive. Like their male colleagues, they preferred men who were well-covered, slim and sensitive-looking.

Women's preferences are also related to personality. Paul Lavrakas in Chicago interviewed a large number of women and found that extrovert, sporty women liked muscular men, while neurotic, radical, drug-using women tended to prefer leaner figures. Traditionally-minded, relatively older women preferred broader figures than younger 'liberated' women. All women preferred the V-shaped physique—slim legs and trunk and a wider upper trunk.

A man's physical attractiveness is apparently not very important to a woman. She places greater weight on other qualities, such as social position and intelligence. At least, that is what she says. The true story may be different, as the next study suggests.

The power of physical attraction

When eligible young people are asked what they would look for in a partner, they mention such qualities as good character, sincerity, warmth and so on. Sexual attractiveness comes well down the list of priorities. In practice, however, they will choose quite differently. Psychologist Elaine Walster set up a computer dance at the University of Minnesota to see who would choose whom. Half-way through the dance everyone was given a questionnaire that asked how much they would like to meet their partner again.

It transpired that physical attractiveness was by far the most important quality, with intelligence and personality well down the list.

Why do people prefer an attractive partner? For one thing, we attribute to attractive people all sorts of positive personality qualities. It also adds to one's status to have an attractive partner. Harold Sigall and David Landy showed that observers impute positive characteristics to a man who is known to have an attractive girl-friend.

Stages of 'courtship'

As in the formation of friendship, there are stages and steps in the development of a romantic relationship.

Stage 1: 'Chatting-up'

Picture a party during which a young man and woman meet each other for the first time and are attracted to each other. According to a New York psychiatrist, Albert Scheflen, they will quite unconsciously go through a number of body changes that bring them into a state of 'readiness'. The muscles of their bodies become slightly tensed, body-sagging disappears and they stand straighter, the man expanding his chest. Stomachs are pulled in and leg muscles tightened. Pupils become dilated, giving a bright-eyed appearance.

As these changes take place, the man or woman may begin to use certain gestures, interpretable as 'preening' behaviour. A woman will stroke her hair, check her make-up or rearrange her clothes. A man may comb his hair, straighten his tie, or perhaps even pull up his socks. As soon as they begin to talk, further changes in gesture and posture will take place: they will arrange their bodies and heads to face one another, lean towards each other and synchronise their postures and gestures in a 'dance' of movement. The man may 'invade' the woman's personal space, or the woman indulge in flirtatious leg movements.

At this stage, the actual meaning of what is said tends to be less important than the non-verbal aspects of both body and voice. Verbally, the couple will be going through stage one of friendship formation—talking about the weather and similar empty topics—to allow body language to come into play. This is a 'face-saving' device, enabling each partner to pick up non-verbal clues of sexual interest or lack of it, saving any undue embarrassment which would result if a verbal message were turned down.

Gerald Clore and his colleagues at the University of Illinois have isolated a number of signals which show how a woman tells a man whether she likes him or not, without saying a word. A woman is seen as warm and accepting if she looks into the man's eyes and smiles with an open mouth, makes movements towards him, touches his hand, uses expressive hand gestures while speaking and looking at his wide-open eyes.

She is seen as uninterested if she gives a 'cold' stare, frowns, looks around the room, looks at her fingernails and behaves in other distracted ways.

An interested male behaves similarly to the warm, responsive female, engaging in a lot of mutual gazing, sitting close and smiling.

The next stage of the relationship will be the 'date'. The initiative for the first date in Western cultures is usually taken by the man, yet covertly it is probably a combined decision. The decisive moment in courtship is the first physical contact, which

*The courtship display
of homo sapiens—
a slow circling dance
with lots of preening.*

in Western society definitely turns the relationship from social to sexual. It is this transition that many men find difficult. Part of the difficulty is because only non-contact signals have been used to express interest up to this point. This has the advantage of being non-committal in the early stage, but they can also be ambiguous. There comes the moment of truth when contact must be made, a risk taken and the chance of rejection faced.

The stage at which the first physical contact occurs varies. There is a lot of misunderstanding between men and women about what they expect to happen on the first date, and what they think their partner expects. In one American study of college students, only half of the men and women actually expected or wanted a kiss after a first date, but nearly three-quarters thought it was expected of them.

As with friendship, the topics discussed get more intimate with each meeting. In addition the level of sexual intimacy will proceed in steps. Desmond Morris divides the sequence into twelve stages, progressing from the first glimpse, right through to copulation. The first three stages involve contact, beginning with hand-touching, maybe in the form of a handshake or disguised as an act of supporting, leading to more intimate exploration of the partner's body. Morris sums it up thus:

eye to body	mouth to mouth
eye to eye	hand to head
voice to voice	hand to body
hand to hand	mouth to breast
arm to shoulder	hand to genitals
arm to waist	genitals to genitals

A more advanced course would also include mouth to genitals.

Stages 5 to 9 on the Morris scale of sexual progression.

The number of steps is arbitrary, but progression through them is probably not. Gerhard Nielsen, working in Copenhagen, also broke the courtship procedure down, finding 24 steps. He suggested that the steps by the man and the counter steps by the girl had a 'coercive order'. For example, when the boy takes the step of holding the girl's hand, he must wait until she presses his hand signalling a go-ahead before he can take the next step.

Nielsen also suggested that a boy or girl is labelled fast or slow in terms of the order of steps—for example, skipping a step—rather than the time taken for each step.

Stage 2: Falling in love

At some point the relationship may progress to the next major stage—falling in love. What does this mean? Is love any more than intensified liking for a person? Zick Rubin found that among dating couples both sexes experienced *love* to a similar degree, but women *liked* their partner rather more than men did. Love meant wanting to be with the lover a lot, being prepared to do almost anything for him and being able to tell him virtually everything. Liking meant thinking the other extremely well-adjusted, having good judgement and having the same things in common. Perhaps men are more romantically inclined than women, in that they have to be in love to have a steady relationship, whereas women may be content to like the partner with whom they go out.

In fact, it seems that the popular belief that women are more romantic than men is wrong, at least when it comes to marriage. The evidence shows that women are more hard-headed about the choice of spouse, going for security and status rather than romance, and inhibiting their true feelings for practical considerations.

For many people there may be quite a sharp difference between liking and loving. Carl Ridley and Arthur Avery asked a large number of young people how important to them the different factors were that make up heterosexual relationships. They found that personal attractiveness and how long the two had known each other mattered for both love and friendship. Lovers, many of whom were engaged, needed sexual intimacy and 'pair solidarity' but *not* what friends needed, intimacy and honesty, confidence and openness.

One of the greatest milestones in the psychology of sex was the publication in 1966 of *Human Sexual Response* by William Masters and Virginia Johnson.[4] They not only described in great detail for the first time what actually happens to the body during love-making, but showed how important the person-to-person process is in leading up to the climax. Most sexual difficulties are not physical, but due to disturbances in this psychological process.

Sex for many people is not an act of love, but quickly and clumsily executed physical release. A central feature of sex 'therapy' is teaching a couple how to take pleasure in themselves and in each other. For the first two stages full intercourse is actually forbidden. The partners take it in turn to caress each other. While one is learning to give pleasure, the other is learning to accept it—a more difficult thing than most people imagine. Learning to give and to experience the sensation of sexual pleasure is important. But this cannot progress properly unless the couple also learn to communicate adequately with each other what they like and do not like. Non-verbal signals—smiles, frowns and noises of pleasure or dissatisfaction—help, but frank speaking is crucial.

8 Assertion and leadership

The ability to influence and control others is essential in most aspects of human relationships, in both informal everyday social contacts and in more formal settings such as work.

Think for a moment what life would be like without these social skills and how serious the consequences would be. If we lack assertive skills we may find ourselves constantly taken advantage of and unable to defend ourselves. This produces timidity and social anxiety which lead us to avoid social situations. This in turn can lead to poor self-esteem and even to feelings of persecution. At work lack of assertiveness can have not only these effects, but can also hinder or prevent promotion. This can jeopardise a person's whole position or at least cause considerable unhappiness, frustration and feelings of inadequacy in the post.

Dominance and competition

Like chickens, monkeys and other animals, men have pecking orders in their groups, with the most dominant ones at the top, the most submissive at the bottom. In animals, dominance leads to priority in eating and choice of sex partners. It is more prominent in males, and is thought to have the biological value of providing leaders who can keep order in the group and repel enemies. Among lower animals, leaders usually maintain their position by physical domination. This makes size and strength very important and it is usually the largest and most mature males who lead. Physical aggression, however, is rare. Competing male animals usually maintain, win or lose their position by threatening postures and gestures, rather than by actual fighting. This perhaps has an evolutionary advantage, by keeping injury and death to a minimum. The superior brain of humans and their sophisticated verbal and non-verbal languages would lead us to expect them to have a completely different means of expressing dominance. This is true in some forms of leadership but in many situations people impress themselves as superior much more by what they do than what they say. In situations of competition and conflict, much use is made of non-verbal signals

Unlike most animals',
man's threat displays
easily topple over into
violence in the
struggle for dominance.

93

for assertion, but among groups of boys actual fighting or the threat of fighting are important.

There seem to be two forms of dominance behaviour, one a display of threatening behaviour used when challenging or being challenged, the other a display of confidence and relaxation shown when the position is secure.

In threatening behaviour, a person speaks with a loud voice, with a lot of expression and variation in pitch. He fixes the other person with a long stare and is the last to look away. He may frown, press his lips tightly together or expose the teeth, or even sneer. He may thrust his head forward in a butting movement, and jut his chin out. He may adopt a threatening posture, described rather whimsically by the American psychiatrist, Albert Scheflen, as a thoracico-lumbar display. More simply,

Unarmed combat, with signs that the arguer on the left will win.

this means toning up the muscles, sticking the chest out, squaring the shoulders, pulling the stomach in and standing tall. He may also stand with arms akimbo—hands on hips with elbows sticking out. Many of these things may be unconsciously designed to make the aggressor *look* bigger. If the aggressor wins the struggle, he will start to wind down, put himself at ease and express the confidence of the victor. This is usually done by relaxing the body, particularly the hands and neck; by leaning back when seated and by casually placed arms and legs. He will also look at the other person *less*, and smile less. This is similar to the behaviour of people in established positions of power and status.

While the dominant person is sending out these signals, he will also be talking more than others, responding very quickly to other people's comments, disagreeing, taking the initiative in changing subjects, and so on.

Soldiers shouted not only into being 'inferior' but into looking subordinate, with stereotyped expressions.

How does a person give away his feelings of inferiority? He is likely to have his chin tucked in, may bite or lick his lips, give a submissive smile (characterised by mouth corners pulled back), look down or away, speak softly and briefly, sit with hands and feet together and shoulders rather slumped.

Someone who is struggling to hold his own in a competitive situation may show his uncertainty by fumbling, stroking his hair or scratching, and twisting his mouth. These and other observations have been made by social scientists such as the British ethologist, Ewan Grant, and American social psychologist Albert Mehrabian.

Self-assertion in everyday life

In the crowded and competitive life of most modern societies, people are perpetually in danger of treading, both literally and metaphorically, on each other's toes, of elbowing each other and in other ways encroaching on each other's territories, and causing, or being caused, offence. Outright aggression is unacceptable as a normal way of protecting one's rights, except under extreme provocation. Equally, giving in to unreasonable actions is to be avoided. Instead, most societies have well-established ways for appropriate self-assertion.

Suppose, for example, John is queueing up in a shop and someone apparently pushes in front of him. John feels angry, grabs the woman by the shoulder, and shouts: 'Hey, just a minute, where do you think you're going? You've got a damned cheek . . .'. This can be highly embarrassing, since the woman may have a good reason for her actions thus putting John totally in the wrong. On the other hand, John could react with resignation, accepting the situation and quietly fuming to himself. He could tell himself it doesn't matter anyway and excuse her by thinking that while it only cost him a couple of minutes, she was probably in a hurry.

There is however a more effective and widely used form of self-assertion, which we will describe below in a series of steps.

First step

John should size up the situation. It may be that the other person has a good excuse. She doesn't realise she has queue-jumped, she may be an assistant taking stock to the other side of the shop, or a customer who has already paid and is making for the nearest exit.

Second step

John should act cautiously to avoid the chance of putting himself in the wrong. A metaphorical or literal 'nudge' to say, 'Did you mean to do that?' may be all that is required to draw the woman's attention to the situation. If she is reasonable, she will apologise or explain what she's doing and move out of the way. If she doesn't, John has to go on to the third step.

Third step

John can now be more explicit and say politely but firmly, 'Excuse me, I was here before you.' This step is clearly more assertive and more clearly a demand, but still leaves open the possibility for the woman to explain herself without putting John in the wrong. If she doesn't excuse herself or refuses to move, John should resort to the fourth step.

Fourth step

John can now demand his rights. He should square up to her, speak in a loud voice and use other signals of the threat display. He can tell her bluntly what she has done, insist on keeping his position, moving himself physically into that position if necessary. But he should never use outright aggression, and this includes verbal abuse.[1]

Leadership skills

One way to become a leader is to have the right qualifications in terms of experience, knowledge and training, and to be appointed from outside the group, for example, by a selection committee. Another way is to emerge as an informal leader of a group from within. Very often, the two are combined. Natural leaders are selected and then trained further.

Supervision of a working group

One of the most important leadership roles in human society is that of the appointed supervisor of a working group in industry, education, government, religion, sport, organised leisure and elsewhere. An appointed leader has power to reward and punish, has a recognised position and plays a particular role within the group. The extent to which he is actually acceptable depends upon his competence, his success in helping the group to attain its goals—for example, industrial productivity—and his concern for group welfare.

Only if he is successful at these things will the group members feel he is entitled to lead and accept his direction. The effects of different leadership skills are considerable. Absenteeism or turnover of staff, for example, can be eight times as much under a very poor leader, and output can slow down eventually to zero.

Basic skills of good leadership

What skills does a good group leader need? First, he needs to get the group working effectively on the task in hand. He must plan the work, set targets, make sure supplies are available, show people how to do it, and win the staff's enthusiasm. However, this has to be done with tact or job satisfaction falls.

Secondly, the good leader looks after the welfare and needs of individual workers, takes a personal interest in them, establishes a friendly relationship with them, is understanding about mistakes, and deals with social problems within the group.

Leaders may be appointed, or simply emerge to dominate larger and larger groups.

Thirdly, he should have the right style of leadership. It is not easy to direct a group and look after it at the same time. Too much direction upsets a friendly relationship, and too much friendliness leads to him losing his authority. The answer is to give direction in a way that doesn't damage the relationship. Explanation and persuasion should be used rather than giving orders. Staff should be allowed to take part in decisions that affect them and group decision techniques should be used. Good leaders lead in a special inconspicuous way.

One common leadership problem is that of group opposition. It is no good trying to persuade individuals, for example asking children in a class to do more homework, if the group has a stronger influence than the leader. One solution is to work through the informal leaders of the group, who may have greater powers of persuasion. Another is to confront the group with the problem and try to bring about a group decision. Difficulties may arise because the would-be leader has forgotten that individual members of the group need to be handled differently, depending on their intelligence, emotional stability, ambition, and so on. Some may respond to a persuasive face-to-face interview, appealing to their own needs or ambitions; others can be handled better by the invention of group rules that apply to all.

Effective leadership takes into account the particular characteristics of the group as well as the tasks to be performed. For example, a more direct and less democratic style would be suited to group members who like authority and are accustomed to firm direction. This is also the most effective style for dealing with crises in which rapid decisions have to be taken, or if the group is large.[2]

Chairmanship of a committee

This is another important leadership role, inside organisations of all kinds. Some committees are mainly set up to be creative, problem-solving groups; others are more concerned with taking decisions that most of those present can agree with. Most committees serve both functions. The committee is a familiar institution with its chairman, secretary, minutes, agenda, rules of procedure, and rather formal speeches. It is quite different from other kinds of group, as is shown by the way those attending a committee may discuss the very same issues at the pub afterwards in a completely different way.

The success of a committee or problem-solving group depends a good deal on the chairman. The chairman should make sure that the committee contains the right people who collectively possess all the skills and knowledge needed for the task. He should ensure that committee discussion goes through a series of cycles: chairman's introduction, provision of information and opinions by members, suggestions about the solution or decision, arriving at a decision or solution. The chairman must direct this to the best advantage. He should summarise the background factors and main arguments on each side, and invite members to express their views.

The effective chairman divides a problem into sub-problems, making use of experts or expert sub-groups to deal with them. He keeps the discussion orderly so that different points are dealt with in turn. He helps the group arrive at a decision by focusing on disagreements and trying to arrive at a creative solution. A characteristic feature of all groups is that a few do most of the talking while the majority remain silent. If the chairman encourages silent members to express their views the quality of solution improves and members are more likely to support the decision taken. Those who talk most tend to be of higher status, but they do not necessarily know most about all the items under discussion and need to be kept under control. Sometimes the first solution to a problem is seized upon by a group, in a kind of instant conformity. If the chairman asks the group to think of a second solution, the group often ends up by preferring it to the first one. Another tendency of groups is to shift towards risky or other extreme judgements, setting aside the original and sounder judgements which individual members had before the discussion began, mainly because they are usually reluctant to appear more conservative than the others. The chairman needs to keep a wary eye out for this too.[3]

Influencing audiences

Public speakers usually aim to influence audiences, to change their attitudes, beliefs or behaviour. They can be very successful: Billy Graham for example persuaded about 4 per cent of the many thousands who attended his meetings in Britain to come forward and 'make decisions'.

For the propagandist type of public speaker prestige is essential.

Crowd-dominators, mind-changers—Julius Caesar, Billy Graham.

He should be seen as an expert, as credible, well-intentioned, as a member of the group, and as attractive. Successful public speakers have charisma based on their intensity, conviction and enthusiasm. They are able to arouse audiences into concern about social conditions, guilt over their wicked life, or whatever is appropriate to the theme, using compelling and dramatic examples or moving stories. The key to persuasion is to link the advocated behaviour with a state of emotional arousal, illustrating how certain behaviour will reduce feelings of anxiety or guilt or resolve some life-long problems.

Appeals may be made directly to the self-interest of the audience (as in politics), or to a person's self-image by a special variety of non-verbal innuendo: 'If you use this kind of petrol, coffee, etc., then you will become that kind of person.'

What the propagandist propagates—uniformity, conformity, unanimity.

The effective propagandist presents his case in a certain order:

1 He makes amiable remarks with which all will agree in order to establish his credentials.
2 He arouses guilt, concern or anxiety.
3 He presents a strong positive case, showing how the feeling aroused can be resolved by the recommended behaviour.
4 He deals with any obvious objections.
5 He draws explicit conclusions and makes recommendations for action.

A public speaker should be in close touch with the audience and sensitive to its reactions. At the same time he should be able to control it, to arouse its concern, and create a strong positive feeling in favour of his proposals. His persuasions will be more effective if he can get the audience to make some kind of decision, engage in some form of public commitment, and become part of a continuing group or organisation.

Lecturers and teachers also need prestige, warmth, enthusiasm and rapport with the audience. They should arouse interest and curiosity rather than emotions. The key to their work is clear exposition of facts, principles and arguments, combined with striking, funny, unusual or otherwise memorable examples.

Different visual aids are extremely useful in producing the right effect. The combination of principle followed by example is very effective. Some repetition is useful, but it is important to vary the materials used. A lecturer should be sensitive to feedback, constantly scanning his audience for signs of boredom or lack of understanding. He should be able to create a total absorption of the group in the topic discussed.

Feedback from the audience for a not-so-good lecturer.

Bargaining and negotiation

In bargaining or negotiation, two sides with different initial preferences aim to arrive at a solution acceptable to both. Examples range from buying and selling, such as bargaining in a North African market, or buying a home where there is no fixed price, to management—union wage-bargaining, international diplomacy, and on a smaller scale, disagreements between husband and wife.

Each side puts forward its demands, followed by a series of concessions with one side usually matching the other. There are persuasive arguments, showing the legitimacy of each side's demands. And there may be tactics involving the use of power, as in industrial relations. There may be collective problem-solving to try to discover the best joint solution.

Each particular kind of negotiation is governed by clearly defined cultural rules about how the whole thing is done. Each side has a target and a limit above or below which it is not prepared to go. One side may have the stronger case, in terms of legitimacy of arguments, or of power. The parties may be primarily concerned to get the best for themselves, or be more concerned to reach agreement.

Bargaining skills

'For you lady (and only for you) I'll knock the price down.'

A negotiator will usually get a better outcome (often at the other's expense) if he has a high target and a high limit. He should conceal or exaggerate his limit, start with extreme demands, and make concessions slowly. (If the other side knows

102

Too low for the seller (left); too high for the buyer; and coming to terms (right).

his real limit, it knows his high demand is bluffing and lower demands should be made.) The side with more time to wait will do better.

In face-to-face negotiations, and when less formal procedures are used, the person with the stronger case does not always win. Interpersonal factors, such as the wish to be thought well of, can interfere. Dean Pruitt has found that the greatest joint profit is obtained when both sides have high targets and high limits, and when they approach the bargaining as a problem to be solved. This can be done by trial-and-error exploration of a number of solutions.[4]

Negotiation can be helped by the services of a mediator. He can suggest a fair compromise and can elicit concessions more readily, since less loss of face is involved. Alternatively, both sides can be represented by junior negotiators. They are less committed to rigid positions, and may be on good terms with each other. The Cuban missile crisis was solved in this way by negotiation between junior diplomats.

Sometimes bargaining moves into a more cooperative discussion of the problem, when each side considers the needs of the other. For this to happen, whether in a marital argument, a strike negotiation or in international diplomacy, it requires a certain degree of trust on either side.

9 Social behaviour in public

In this chapter we turn to the way we behave in public, with comparative strangers, in the street, in shops, in libraries, in crowds, and elsewhere. People relate to strangers by special kinds of bodily behaviour to enable them to make joint use of space, and they behave in accordance with formal roles. Their behaviour is affected by social class, and by cultural differences between people.

City life with its ever-changing collection of strangers requires a special set of social skills. We share the same space and cooperate over the use of shared facilities. We use the same pavements without bumping into one another. When passing on the pavement two people will look at each other at a distance of twelve feet or more, acknowledging each other's presence, and seeing enough to avoid a collision. Closer than this, they avert gaze in what Erving Goffman called 'civil inattention'. This signals that there is not going to be a social encounter.

Peter Collett and Peter Marsh videotaped people crossing the road at a crowded zebra crossing. They found that:

1 In London (where cars drive on the left) people cross to the right.
2 If they are going *left* they give a definite bodily signal to indicate this, and
3 Men cross with the fronts of their bodies to the other, women with their backs.

When in public, we take great pains to prevent our behaviour appearing bizarre or incomprehensible. For example, we feel that a sudden turn-about is disconcerting, unless we accompany it by gestures indicating that we have forgotten something. This is what Goffman described as 'body gloss'.

People in the street do not normally speak to strangers. If someone wants to ask the way, he has to approach another person, catch his eye, apologise or seek permission to converse and speak. The beginning and ending is signalled by a bodily movement, which we all recognise unconsciously.

We all have about 0·9 square metre of *personal space*. We prefer others, especially strangers, to keep out of this area. In a largely

Sharing out the space: even in crowds and under pressure, we manage to preserve our 'room'.

deserted library if a person takes a seat alongside another person the latter will often move away. The same thing happens when the new arrival stares persistently at the other person thus invading his visual space. Motorists have been found to move on more swiftly from traffic lights when being stared at by a bystander.

Two people indicate that they are together by their proximity; their relationship is shown by their closeness, bodily contact, and other non-verbal signals. Verbal signals also work. Experiments show that few people will walk between two others who are talking. Try talking to a friend across the width of a pavement, and you will find that passers-by will carefully walk round you. In a group the most popular or most influential member is usually in the middle, with the less well-accepted members on the outside—physically as well as socially. An area may be defended against invasion by leaving coats, books or other property round it, or by sitting in the middle of the long side of the table, facing the direction from which invasion might come.

Queue-forming is a common feature of public behaviour in certain countries. There are special rules about behaviour in queues, especially those that last a long time. In Australia, Leon Mann studied all-night queues outside football grounds.[1] He found that some people operated in shifts, each person doing one hour on and two to three hours off; others staked their claim by leaving boxes or beds, but such places could be kept only for two to three hours, after which the property was smashed up. Boxes were also used as barriers to keep out infiltrators.

Close bodily proximity is another feature of queues. On elevators, buses, and Underground trains as well as in crowds, people seem to forget about their need for personal space. In these conditions we treat one another to some extent as objects. We do not speak or look at each other, and no social signals are exchanged, so that the problem of too much intimacy does not arise.

Territorial defence achieved, for up to two hours, by 'deposit'.

Formal behaviour

*When there is a strong
focus of mass attention,
personal territories
are forgotten (above).*

Much public behaviour is not spontaneous, but governed by rules, standard patterns of interaction and ritual.

Roles

In a hospital, there are defined *positions*—patient, nurse, doctor, visitor—each position having its special clothes, behaviour, and special relationships with those in the other positions. These *roles* are interlocking, so that patients and nurses adopt complementary styles of behaviour. Roles also carry different amounts of *power*, and make up a *communication system*; doctors rarely speak to visitors, for example.

A certain degree of latitude is allowed within roles, particularly for higher-status roles, such as that of doctor. But to some extent members of organisations have to suppress their spontaneous style, or at least learn to express it within the limits of the role. This may lead to conflict between personality and role. Some American students, for instance, have been found to drift away from universities to military academies offering roles more suited to their personalities.

In society, we play our roles as males or females of a certain age group and a certain social class. We all signal our status,

107

occupation and other roles by appearance, accent, style of behaviour, or in words. There are special ways in which middle-class, middle-aged males behave, and in which they relate to those in the other categories. An industrial foreman can clearly be distinguished by his clothes from workers or managers. One can also tell from his appearance whether he sees himself as one of the workers or one of the managers.

Roles sometimes prescribe the nature of an interaction in some detail. For example, the conversation between a customer and a shop assistant, a waiter, or a bank clerk, can only follow a certain rather standardised course. There are as many as 800 simple, everyday encounters like this, including going to the supermarket, catching a bus, going to church and many more. To be a competent member of society it is necessary to have mastered them.

Rituals

Rituals are standardised patterns of social behaviour which are symbolic rather than instrumental. A handshake doesn't do anything to another's hand, but stands for a change of relationship or of accessibility. The French anthropologist, Van Gennep, divided rituals like weddings into three phases: 'separation' (e.g., of a bride from her family), 'transition' (the period of the wedding), and 'incorporation' (setting up home with her husband or his family).

Non-verbal signals play an important part. For example, the power of a priest or other official is accentuated by laying on of hands, or by symbolic acts like putting on the chain of office, or spilling red paint to represent menstrual blood in the primitive healing of barrenness.

The Masai moran *must undergo a dangerous 'rite of passage' on his way to manhood.*

Social class

Strict rituals observed in the Japanese 'tea ceremony' (above, left) and in the sunset lighting of candles for the Jewish sabbath (above).

Whether we like it or not, social class is one of the main ways in most societies in which people differ.

Social class greatly affects relationships between people. We tend to spend most of our time with people of our own class, when we are with family, friends and at leisure but not at work, where the work-role relationship matters more than class difference. Different social classes also come into contact in formal relations such as at the doctor's, in shops, and so on.

Informal relations across classes are rare. They are seen, for example, when someone asks a stranger the direction in the street. Mary Sissons carried out an experiment at Paddington Station, London, in which an actor dressed himself up as upper-middle-class in the morning, and working-class in the afternoon, with accents to match. He asked 80 people the way to Hyde Park and the encounters were filmed and analysed.

It was found that middle-class respondents spent longer talking to the actor in his middle-class role, and also smiled more. There appeared to be an immediate rapport between middle-class people. With either interviewer they gave a definite ending to the encounter by smiling, looking and nodding, whereas the working-class respondents simply walked away. There was not much evidence of the commonly assumed deferential behaviour to those of higher social class.

There are interesting class differences in speech style. Basil Bernstein[2] of London University has found that working-class people use shorter sentences, often unfinished and make frequent use of personal pronouns with what appear to be questions ('didn't I?'). Peter Robinson studied how mothers answered children's questions, and concluded that these styles of speaking are passed on to children by their mothers. Bernstein argues that the working-class speech is adapted to maintain relationships within face-to-face cooperative groups. It seeks constant social responses, while the middle-class 'elaborated' code is more impersonal, depends less on local idiom and is more appropriate for administration and impersonal decision-taking.

Class differences are found in methods of child-rearing, which give rise to differences in personality, such as middle-class concern with achievement and long-term goals. Middle-class parents tend to make more use of reasoning and explanation and to teach their children to think about the consequences of their behaviour. They use less physical punishment and make fewer direct commands or threats and they emphasise waiting for rewards later rather than spending a lot of money now. Combined with the more elaborate use of language, this results in more inner-direction of behaviour, putting plans into words and long-term goals.

Class systems vary from country to country. The Indian caste system is an interesting variety with no mobility between castes, and physical distances allowed between members of one caste and another strictly defined. European countries have moved away from the earlier feudal relationships. Today there is more social mobility but *less* contact between classes, and big differences still in wealth, status and life-styles. In Britain a new class of 'affluent workers' has appeared with 'middle-class' prosperity but lower-class attitudes and outlook. In the USA and Australia, although there is emphasis on 'equality', and easier inter-class contacts, there are still great differences in wealth between classes.

Cultural differences

Interaction with members of other cultural groups can raise various problems. They may be racial minority groups in one's own country, foreigners encountered through business, visitors from abroad, or those met while travelling. Their unfamiliar behaviour can give rise to dislike, misunderstanding, avoidance and even to a feeling that they are not really human.

There are several areas of social behaviour in which cultural differences have been found.

Non-verbal communication

The *same* signals can convey different meanings in different cultures. Touch has a different significance in 'contact cultures' where touch is common, from 'non-contact cultures', and this can cause a lot of misunderstanding. The Arabs, for example, not

Gift-giving can ease the difficulties of transcultural meetings.

only touch during conversation but stand much closer, face one another directly, and gaze more. This can cause a Westerner to move backwards and sideways as he is pursued in a wide circle by an Arab interlocutor. The Japanese show little emotion in the face, and rarely display negative emotions; we found that Japanese, subjects could recognise emotions from facial expressions of Englishmen more readily than from those of their fellow Japanese even though the British tend to conceal their feelings and often writhe inwardly in situations where Italians or Arabs might shout or weep. Italians make far more use of gesture to illustrate and amplify their speech. Blacks in the USA seem to use a different pattern of looking during conversation—they look less while listening, whereas whites look more—so that both sides may think the other isn't attending. Frederick Erickson at Harvard found that this led white interviewers to produce simpler explanations of what they had just said since they thought the black interviewee hadn't understood the first time.

111

Verbal communication

Language barriers do not only mean new words and grammar. They can be more subtle, involving different ways of using language. For example, in Ireland and the Middle East, there is a polite use of language, aimed to please the hearer rather than to convey accurate information. In Britain, middle-class people are often modest about their achievements, while in some other countries they exaggerate them. Both tendencies can be equally misleading.

In Japan, one does not ask direct questions unless quite sure that the answer will be 'yes' because saying 'no' causes loss of face. In America, the polite way of giving an order—'Would you like to . . .?'—can often be mistaken for a question by a foreigner. And the French system of personal pronouns (*tu*, *vous*) like our use of first names, often signals both intimacy and status in subtle ways.

Ideas

Each culture has words to reflect the way it looks upon the world. The rainbow is divided up differently with differently named 'colours' in different cultures. There may be one or several words for different kinds of rice, snow—or pyschologists—if these divisions are important in a culture. There may be concepts whose full meaning may be difficult for an outsider to grasp. We no longer attach much meaning to 'honour', for example, but have some new concepts, such as 'cool', 'weird', 'far-out'.

Rules and conventions

Rules governing different social situations can vary sharply from one culture to another. Kenneth Pike, at the University of Michigan, reported the case of an American missionary girl who found herself in difficulties with a cannibal chief when she tried to throw him on the floor (shake hands) and laughed at him (smiled).

Visitors to other cultures are often confused by unfamiliarity with the rules about gifts. Buying and selling are dictated by rules barter. They must learn what is proper to eat and drink, and how to deal with the opposite sex without causing offence. Other special situations, complete with rules, may not exist in the home culture.

Moral values

There are a number of important areas where cultures differ in their moral codes, ideals and beliefs. Telling the truth is regarded as fairly unimportant in a number of cultures. Norms of sexual behaviour vary between cultures as well as between generations. Aggressiveness is approved of in cultures where war is common and defence of the homeland important. A particular life-style may be valued—for example, the spontaneous, relaxed and happy disposition of the Italian in contrast with the self-disciplined, hard-working and puritanical 'Protestant ethic'. Milton Rokeach found that there is more prejudice towards people with different morals and beliefs than towards those of a different colour.

Social structure

The relations between social classes, men and women, and different age groups also vary between cultures, giving rise to inter-cultural problems. Americans often find other countries more hierarchical than their own, in the amount of deference shown to senior members of organisations. In many countries women do not participate as equals, or may be jealously guarded; old people may be greatly revered. Certain groups are rejected and despised, such as the Indian 'untouchable' caste. Travellers who find themselves in contact with a new culture can find themselves inadvertently causing trouble by breaking the rules or by signalling that they intend to transgress even when they do not mean to do so. Their self-image can also be quite seriously disturbed, leading to the condition known as 'culture shock'.

A form of social skills' training for behaviour in other cultures has been devised by psychologists at the University of Illinois.[3] Known as the 'Culture Assimilator', it is based on incidents where Americans have got into difficulties in, for example, Thailand. The method gives training in ideas, conventions and values relating to such customs as the giving and receiving of gifts, entertaining guests and dealing with women.

Helpfulness and concern for others

Helpful behaviour and concern for others may appear paradoxical to those psychologists who tend to assume that behaviour is directed towards satisfying one's own needs, not someone else's. Nevertheless there are good grounds for thinking that concern for others is a basic part of human, and indeed animal, nature. When a monkey in a cage has a lot of bananas and a monkey in the next cage has none, he will often spontaneously share his fruit. Even when he does not do so unprompted, he will probably respond to begging by the other. Chimpanzees, it has been remarked, seem to find it quite hard to refuse requests from their fellows to share.

Elsewhere in this series you can read about Stanley Milgram's famous (or infamous) experiment in which he found that some people who considered themselves to be under orders were prepared to deliver lethal electric shocks to a man for making mistakes. But other researchers such as R. F. Weiss and colleagues, discovered that people will find it rewarding to turn off an electric shock that someone else is suffering when there is 'nothing in it' for them at all.[4]

Childhood experiences also affect an individual's concern for others. If parents encourage and reward altruistic behaviour the child comes to associate helping others with being rewarded. If a person is profusely thanked for telling someone the way, he is more than twice as likely to help another person pick up a dropped bag immediately afterwards than if the thanks are merely formal. Imitation is also very important. If a collector for charity first approaches an assistant who is seen to give generously, the next person approached is much more likely to be generous—a principle familiar to fund-raisers. The example of others proves to be much more effective than moral exhortation (especially if the others don't practise what they preach).

People help more if this is general practice in their group or community. In some cultures it is expected that individuals like doctors or teachers will help those for whom they are responsible, or where it is their duty. Elsewhere there is a norm of reciprocity, and some gift, or as we would say, 'bribe', is expected.

Norms also inhibit helpfulness. In Britain and America, an individual is much less likely to help someone in trouble if there are a lot of bystanders doing nothing, since there appears to be a norm of indifference. This has both been found in experiments and observed in such real events as in the notorious case of the stabbing of a girl named Kitty Genovese in New York in 1969 in full view of 38 people, none of whom came to help or even called the police.

A group of bystanders is less likely to help a fallen man than a single passer-by—but they would quickly follow the Samaritan's example.

Which kinds of people are most helpful? We have seen that childhood experiences are important.

A person is more likely to help someone if he has experienced the other's trouble himself. Peter Burley at Oxford found that helpful people were high in 'social intelligence', that is, they were able to perceive the thoughts and feelings of others accurately and to understand social behaviour. Other studies have found that people help more in familar situations, where they know what to do. Helping others effectively is not only a matter of goodwill, but often requires expert knowledge or skill.

Deviant groups

If a person deviates from important social norms, he is likely to be rejected by many people. If a group of people deviate together, they can form a group in which members are accepted, despite public opinion. Deviant groups include racial minority groups, homosexuals, drug addicts and those who are physically deformed.

Those who are not satisfied with regular community life may be motivated to join a deviant group which offers friendship, a new identity, fun and excitement, as well as any particular gratifications offered by the group. New members may have to be 'socialised' into the group, taught how to smoke pot and how to feel 'high', for example, if the group is one of drug addicts. There may be a 'career' inside the deviant group with a progression through different grades of seniority. Peter Marsh, a psychologist at Oxford, found that the famous British football hooligans are far from being the delinquents that mass media stereotypes have made them into. They have a distinct order with different ranks, each with its special style of dress. The real troublemakers, the 'nutters' are outsiders even from this group of 'outsiders'.

Deviants have to be recognised and labelled by others before they can be rejected or otherwise reacted to as outsiders. This labelling can affect the self-image of those labelled, like those who chant 'we are the famous football hooligans'.

On the other hand, when groups *are* clearly recognisable their labelling by the police and news media may bring about 'deviance amplification'. They come to accept the extreme stereotypes held about themselves and may become cut off from the rest of society, falling outside normal processes of social control. This was reported about drug-taking groups in the 1960s, who became increasingly isolated and increasingly deviant in their life-style.

10 Social failure

Let us now take a look at Mr Able who is adept at the social skills that we have described and compare him with Mr Awkward, a typical social bumbler.

Mr Able begins an informal encounter with a familiar but social raising of the brows and a wave. He approaches and takes up a certain stance at two to four feet from his companion, depending on the relationship between them. After an exchange of salutations and pleasantries, Mr Able asks questions and rewards the other for speaking, with head nods, grunts, smiles and verbal comments. From time to time he takes up the conversation, aiming to speak between one-third and two-thirds of the time. While he speaks he sends a continual stream of non-verbal signals, glances, movements of the brows, the head, shifts in posture and gesture. He constantly changes volume, pitch and pace to give meaning and emphasis.

If Mr Able is feeling friendly he expresses this by smiling and making eye contact. He leans forward in an open posture and adopts a fairly soft tone of voice. When two people are really close they will indulge, without consciousness, in a kind of sychronised dance of movements, swaying backwards and forwards and mirroring each other's movements. If he were feeling dominant he would either sit erect with shoulders squared and head high, or loll at a reclining angle, with limbs sprawled out. He would at times stare the other down, and at other times look away or through the other, interrupt him, ask a lot of questions and give advice. He would also take all the initiatives in starting and ending the conversation and changing topics.

Mr Awkward, on the other hand, does few or none of these things. When approaching an acquaintance, he looks studiously at his feet and walks on. If stopped and greeted he may still fail to look up, and only manage a low mumble by way of acknowledgement. When seated in company he may sit apart from the others, with his body turned away and his head down, face blank, shoulders slumped and arms and legs crossed. When questioned, he replies in monosyllables in a dreary tone and in a voice often too low to hear. He is very hard to get through to, and people tend to feel that it is just not worth the effort.

Mr Able enters a situation with a motive. He wants to make a new friend, to make an impression, to sell something or just to fill in five minutes pleasantly. He has a plan, though not necessarily

The behaviour of
someone socially
ill at ease
will tend to reinforce
his exclusion: he offers
no 'reward' to others.

a conscious one, about how to achieve his goal. He sizes up the situation, reads the social signals, and decides on a line of action. From his repertoire of skills he chooses one which he thinks will have the desired effect; to dominate, persuade, seduce or provoke. Having acted, he will watch the effect, and act accordingly, perhaps changing his tactic, deploying another skill. From his experience of many previous situations, Mr Able knows what is expected of him in a given situation—such as polite conversation at a cocktail party, or addressing his questions to the chairman at a meeting. Knowing the rules, he uses them to his best advantage, just as a chess-player will use the rules to win the game.

Mr Awkward has no real motive or plan. He fails to pick up subtle non-verbal messages, since he usually averts his gaze when in company. He has a limited repertoire of skills and is quite unaware of the effect of his own behaviour. Mr Awkward sends out negative signals of coldness or hostility, which he does not intend but which result in avoidance or rejection by others. The result is that he labels others as unfriendly and mean, finds social encounters increasingly difficult and painful, and will end up withdrawing into his shell, where he sits, mopes, becomes depressed and even suicidal.

A number of experimental studies have shown that many mental patients are not mentally ill at all but are suffering from various kinds of failure in social skills. Some never learned them. Others become so anxious in social situations that their skills fail them. Still others are only able to express one message, whatever they really feel. For instance, certain people are very good at dominating others, but hopeless at showing love and friendliness. Others are likeable and popular, but have no authority and get pushed around.

Expressiveness

We have seen that body language is much more powerful than ordinary verbal language at expressing feelings and attitudes, like anger and joy, liking, love and dominance. Failure can happen in two ways. Either there is a failure to use body language at all, with blank, expressionless and still posture; or the wrong message is sent, for example seductiveness instead of shyness, or hostility instead of annoyance. In the first case people say they *want* to communicate but just can't. In the second they believe that they are communicating, but are wrong about the messages they are sending. They have little or no awareness of their effect on others.

Conversation

Conversation needs a listener and a speaker; failure in either role will result in the conversation breaking down. Many of these patients are poor listeners. They give no feedback to the person speaking. They fail to adopt the listener-posture, to look enough, or to nod, smile and give verbal comments.

They are also poor talkers. They speak very briefly (10 per cent or less of the time) and about topics which are boring (like the

The man on the left
excludes attention
by 'blinkering' himself
with his hands.

weather) or inappropriate and embarrassing ('my sex life is hopeless', or 'my operation . . .'). There is little variety in what they talk about and an absence of humour. They do not know how to adjust the amount of information to their listener's interest. Topics couched in such general terms that it is difficult to get any detailed information—or there is so much detail that others find it tiresome to listen to them. Some patients never express an opinion or a feeling and do not disclose things about themselves; while others can *only* talk about themselves and their problems, monopolising the conversation, continually interrupting and showing no interest in the other person. Finally, some specialise in interrogating others, making very personal comments, disagreeing and criticising, even with a complete stranger.

Non-verbal signals complement verbal ones in various ways, including managing turns at speaking. Some of our patients notably fail to do this in the following ways. They do not hand over the conversation with questions and a shift in posture and gaze. They do not use the non-verbal equivalents of full-stops, so others do not know when they have finished talking. They fail to send out starting signals, so others never know when they want to speak. What is more, they do not observe the turn-taking cues given by others. The result is poor meshing, marked by periods of awkward silence on the one hand and frequent interruptions on the other.

There are other problems too. Some speak so softly that it is a strain to listen. When they talk there is a lack of variation in pitch, volume and speed—essential for emphasis and non-verbal punctuation—resulting in dullness and confusion about the meaning of statements. For instance, while normal speakers use non-verbal cues to show that their speech is intended to be funny, sarcastic, or serious, patients often do not, leaving the listener uncertain and uncomfortable about how to respond: Is he being serious? Am I supposed to laugh or what?

Rewardingness
Poor communicators are seen by others as unrewarding. Because they fail to respond and give feedback, they also fail in those small but vital pleasantries of everyday life, such as smiling, agreeing and supporting with nods and other affirmatives; showing that they understand by reflecting back; taking an interest in the other; thanking, praising, complimenting, offering sympathy and help, giving things, offering invitations. They often fail to make amends when they interrupt, by not apologising or offering an explanation. They fail to respond to the other's smile or offer of help or support, leaving the other feeling slighted or even offended.

The uncommunicativeness of Korchnoi and Spaski safeguards each from 'giving himself away'.

Influence and control
Poor communicators lack the skills of assertion and control. They rarely initiate encounters, but find it difficult to part when in one. They do not change the topic of conversation, or put an alternative point of view or give advice. They also find it difficult or impossible to make requests, let alone demands, or to complain, criticise, persuade others or make suggestions.

Self-presentation

Many of these patients present themselves poorly; for instance, by being too modest or dwelling on negative things about themselves. A few over-present and work too hard at it, boasting loudly to comparative strangers. Other patients present themselves inappropriately. One girl student, for example, dressed and sounded like someone 40 years older. Others present a different kind of false front, and pretend to be something they are not, and may actually know very little about.

Some of our socially-phobic patients are afraid of failure in self-presentation, such as shaking, blushing or being sick at a formal dinner. Some people come to us with this problem, whom nobody else would ever guess had any such trouble. One rich industrialist, who was very skilled in leadership at board meetings, had a terror that his social self would suddenly collapse, that he would have a panic attack at a party which would completely destroy his public image.

Training in social skills

People who lack basic social skills will not be helped much by talking about their problems or by having their symptoms treated. They need a method of learning new skills.[1]

The normal way of learning these skills takes 20 years or more during growing up. A training programme must take rather less than this: say 20 hours! From the limited research available, three processes seem particularly important.

Instruction

Parents tell their children quite explicitly how to behave: 'Say hello ... Say goodbye ... Say thank you ... Look at me ... Don't interrupt'. Teenagers instruct each other on what they think are the best strategies, for instance, of chatting up someone of the opposite sex. By the same token social-skill therapists give a good deal of simple instruction. Patients are given lessons in how to use their eyes, on what to say to open a conversation in a friendly manner. They are shown video tapes of themselves in action, and are often stunned to see how they really appear to other people.

Modelling

Most people aspire at various times in their lives to be like someone they admire. Small boys and girls emulate their parents in role-playing games like Mothers and Fathers. As we grow older, we copy competent (and sometimes, unfortunately, not so competent) peers, particularly older ones. Many inadequate people have had ineffective parents, or have lacked a peer group during the crucial formative years. In a therapy group the therapist acts out moods, emotions and conversation. Members of the group take it in turns to practise and learn from each other.

Reinforcement

Both instruction and modelling operate partly by reinforcement. Approved behaviour is rewarded, and disapproved behaviour is either punished or ignored. In a therapy session the therapist will always reward the person warmly for the behaviour he wants to encourage. The reward may be a simple remark like, 'Well done!', or it may be the same with the addition of a warm smile and a hand on the shoulder.

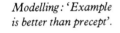

Modelling: 'Example is better than precept'.

Often the reward will come spontaneously when perhaps for the first time in his or her life the person finds others responding naturally. Someone who has spent his life scowling at others out of fear may never have received a smile as a response to any behaviour on his part. When the therapist has shown him what his behaviour looks like, has taught him, piece by piece, new ways of behaving, and he begins to feel the new self growing, that new experience can be a powerful reward in itself.

A smile and a pat on the back are not rewards for everybody, however. Some of our patients have to learn to respond to the social reinforcers. For instance, the person we have just described may have never won a smile from anybody else by his own actions—unless they were mocking or teasing him—but is highly likely to have been on the receiving end of smiles not related directly to him. Perhaps he passed someone in the street who had just had good news and who was smiling at everybody who passed. Smiles would have come to him at random. There would have been no rule to them, and so they would have been meaningless. This person would have to learn in the group that smiles mean something, that they are tokens of friendliness and approval.

In such ways old patterns of behaviour can be changed or completely obliterated, and new ways established to replace them. The person will become a new person as his experience of himself and the world changes, and as his social world opens up. The method is quicker and probably more effective than many forms of psychotherapy, because it strikes at the immediate problem—what passes from person to person.

References

1   Elements of social behaviour

1. Ekman, P., Friesen, W. V. and Ellsworth, P. *Emotions in the Human Face.* Elmsford, NY: Pergamon, 1972.
2. Argyle, M. and Cook, M. *Gaze and Mutual Gaze.* Cambridge University Press, 1976.
3. Mehrabian, A. *Nonverbal Communication.* Chicago: Aldine-Atherton, 1972.
4. Hall, E. T. *The Hidden Dimension.* Garden City, NY: Doubleday, 1960.

2   The two languages of humans

1. Argyle, M. et al. 'The communication of inferior and superior attitudes by verbal and non-verbal signals'. *Brit. J. soc. clin. Psychol.*, 1970, 9, 221–231.
2. Argyle, M. *The Psychology of Interpersonal Behaviour.* Harmondsworth: Penguin Books, 1978 (3rd edition).
3. Marsh, P., Rosser, E. and Harré, R. *The Rules of Disorder.* London: Routledge & Kegan Paul, 1978.

3   Judging other people; believing is seeing

1. Kleinke, C. L. *First Impressions.* Englewood Cliffs, NJ: Prentice Hall, 1975.
2. Cook, M. *Interpersonal Perception.* Harmondsworth: Penguin Books, 1971.
3. Jones, E. E., Kanouse, D. E., Kelley, H. H., Nisbett, R. E., Valins, S. and Weiner, B. *Attribution: Perceiving the causes of behaviour.* Morristown: General Learning Press, 1971.

4   Analysing conversation

1. Duncan, S. and Fiske, D. W. *Face-to-Face Interaction.* Hillsdale, NJ: Erlbaum, 1977.
2. Weizenbaum, J. *Computer Power and Human Reason.* San Francisco: Freeman, 1967.
3. Kendon, A. and Ferber, A. 'A description of some human greetings'. In R. P. Michael and J. H. Crook (Eds.) *Comparative Ecology and the Behaviour of Primates.* London: Academic Press, 1973.

5   Persons and situations

1. Wish, M. and Kaplan, S. J. 'Toward an implicit theory of interpersonal communication'. *Sociometry,* 1975, 40, 234–246.
2. Eysenck, H. J. and Eysenck, S. B. G. *Personality Structure and Measurement.* London: Routledge & Kegan Paul, 1969.
3. Argyle, M. 'Personality and social behaviour'. In R. Harré (Ed.) *Personality.* Oxford: Blackwell, 1976.

6   A sense of self

1. Erikson, E. H. 'The problem of ego identity'. *Amer. J. Psychoanalysis,* 1956, 4, 56–121.
2. Duval, S. and Wicklund, R. A. *A Theory of Objective Self Awareness.* NY: Academic Press, 1972.
3. Goffman, E. *The Presentation of Self in Everyday Life.* Edinburgh University Press, 1956.
4. Hurlock, E. B. 'Motivation in fashion'. *Arch. Psychol.,* 1929, *111*, 1–72.

7   Friendship and love

1. Duck, S. *The Study of Acquaintance.* Farnborough, Hants:
   Saxon House, 1977.
2. Byrne, D. *The Attraction Paradigm.* NY: Academic Press, 1971.
3. Morris, D. *Intimate Behaviour.* London: Cape, 1971.
4. Masters, W. H. and Johnson, V. E. *Human Sexual Response.*
   Boston: Little, Brown, 1966.

8   Assertion and leadership

1. Bower, S. A. and Bower, G. H. *Assert Yourself.* Reading,
   Mass.: Addison-Wesley, 1976.
2. Argyle, M. *The Social Psychology of Work.* Harmondsworth:
   Penguin Books, 1972.
3. Hoffman, L. R. 'Group problem-solving'. *Advances in Experimental
   Social Psychology*, 1965, *2*, pp. 99–132.
4. Pruitt, D. G. 'Power and Bargaining'. In B. Seidenberg and
   A. Snadowsky (Eds.) *Social Psychology.* NY: Free Press, 1976.

9   Social behaviour in public

1. Mann, L. 'The social psychology of waiting lines'. *American
   Scientist*, 1970, *58*, 390–398.
2. Bernstein, B. 'A public language: some sociological implications
   of a linguistic form'. *British Journal of Sociology*, 1959, *10*, 311–326.
3. Fiedler, F. E., Mitchell, T. and Triandis, H. C. 'The culture
   assimilator: an approach to cross-cultural training'.
   Journal of Applied Psychology, 1971, *55*, 95–102.
4. Weiss, R. F., Buchanan, W., Alstaff, L. and Lombardo, J. P.
   'Altruism is rewarding'. *Science*, 1971, *171*, 1262–1263.

10   Social failure

1. Trower, P., Bryant, B. and Argyle, M. *Social Skills and Mental
   Health.* London: Methuen, 1971.

Suggested further reading

Argyle, M. (1978) *The Psychology of Interpersonal Behaviour.* Harmondsworth:
   Penguin Books, 3rd edition.
Argyle, M. (1975) *Bodily Communication.* London: Methuen, New York: Inter-
   national Universities Press.
Baron, R. A. and Byrne, D. (1977) *Social Psychology*, Boston: Allyn and Bacon,
   2nd edition.
Coulthard, M. (1977) *Discourse Analysis.* London: Longman.
Galassi, M. D. and Galassi, J. P. (1977) *Assert Yourself: How to be your own
   person.* New York, London: Human Sciences Press.
Goffman, E. (1971) *Relations in Public.* London: Allen Lane.
Harper, R. G., Wiens, A. N. and Matarazzo, J. D. (1978) *Nonverbal Communication.*
   New York: Wiley.
Trower, P., Bryant, B., and Argyle, M. (1978) *Social Skills and Mental
   Health.* London: Methuen, Pittsburgh University Press.
Wrightman, L. S. (1977) *Social Psychology.* Monterey, Calif: Brooks/Cole.

Index

Photo credits